MY PARENT HAS CANCER AND IT REALLY SUCKS

REAL-LIFE ADVICE FROM REAL-LIFE TEENS

MAYA SILVER & MARC SILVER

sourcefire

This book is not intended as a substitute for medical advice from a qualified physician. The intent of this book is to provide accurate general information in regard to the subject matter covered. If medical advice or other expert help is needed, the services of an appropriate medical professional should be sought.

All brand names and product names used in this book are trademarks, registered trademarks, or trade names of their respective holders. Sourcebooks, Inc., is not associated with any product or vendor in this book.

Published by Sourcebooks Fire, an imprint of Sourcebooks, Inc.
P.O. Box 4410, Naperville, Illinois 60567-4410
(630) 961-3900
Fax: (630) 961-2168
teenfire.sourcebooks.com

Library of Congress Cataloging-in-Publication Data

Silver, Marc
  My parent has cancer and it really sucks / Marc Silver, Maya Silver.
    pages cm
  Audience: Grade 9 to 12.
  1. Children of cancer patients—Juvenile literature. 2. Cancer—Psychological aspects—Juvenile literature. I. Silver, Maya. II. Title.
  RC264.S52 2013
  616.99'4—dc23

                              2012039095

          Printed and bound in the United States of America.
                  VP 10 9 8 7 6 5 4 3 2 1

To the amazing Anna Gottlieb,
who told us we had to write this book

And to Marsha, who taught us that cancer sucks,
tolerated two clueless teens and one clueless husband,
and motivated us to write this guide

Contents

INTRODUCTION

Dear Teens (and Parents),

Many, many teens have faced a parent's cancer. An estimated 2.85 million American children live with a parent who is a cancer survivor, according to the authors of "Parental Cancer and the Family," a paper published recently in the journal *Cancer*. In the households surveyed, more than a third of the children were ages twelve to seventeen.

Those teenagers are an "unheard group," says oncology counselor Shara Sosa. "They have a lot of needs." But there's not a lot of attention paid.

Teens, this book is for you.

You may recognize yourself in the pages ahead—your worries, your fears, your optimism, your pessimism, your anger, your sense of humor, your feelings of despair, your hopefulness. That's because we talked to more than one hundred teenagers all across the country.

While no two teens are alike, you'll probably find voices that echo your thoughts and feelings, providing a sense of comfort (like that feeling you get when you find out someone else likes the same weird movie as you do).

You'll also come upon insights that might give you a different perspective on what you're going through (like when you discover a new band and it rocks your world).

We talked to many experts as well—doctors, therapists, guidance counselors, chaplains who counsel teens coping with a parent's cancer—to give you an assortment of top-notch advice.

We even talked to some parents. (Don't worry, they won't tell you to do your homework or pick up the junk on your bedroom floor.)

We also talked about our own experiences as the husband and daughter of a breast cancer survivor. You can read some of our conversations in sections called "Marc says" and "Maya says."

We hope that the voices in this book create a community of support to give you strength as you deal with your parent's cancer. Because if you can learn from the 20/20 hindsight and mistakes of others who've been there, you'll be better prepared to handle the situations you will encounter.

A parent's cancer is uncharted territory, and the uncertainty about what's happening and what's next can be nerve-racking. "Among the things I wish I was told with more clarity is: here's what your mom's going to be going through, here's what you need to do, what you need to be aware of..." said Aaron, who was a teen when his mom had breast cancer. This book doesn't have all the answers, but it will provide you with an idea of what might be going on—and how to get the information you need if your parents aren't good communicators.

One of the most important things we learned from interviewing so many teens—and one of the themes of this guide—is that everyone deals with their parent's cancer differently.

Some people cope just fine. Others have a very hard time. A lot depends on the nature of the diagnosis. Is your parent facing a cancer that has a good treatment success rate? Or is the cancer a difficult one to treat?

Your reaction also depends on you. Personalities differ. Some teens want lots and lots of information. Others want the bare minimum. Some worry a great deal. Others feel confident that everything will be okay. Some lose their focus at school and see grades slip. Others hyper-focus on keeping grades up. Some want to talk about it all. Others don't. And that's okay.

One thing we can all agree on, though, is that cancer sucks. For everyone involved. We hope this book will help you cope in the months and years ahead.

As hard as times may get, you will make it through. Take it from Bailee Richardson, who was twelve when her mom was diagnosed: "Stay strong. Everything's going to work itself out in the end. Don't ever let it get the best of you."

Finally, here are two rules for this book:

Rule 1: Teens, don't feel guilty. You have your own way of coping, and you don't have to behave like any other teen in this book.

Rule 2: Parents, do not use the book to make your teen talk if he or she doesn't want to talk.

Read on!

NOTE FOR PARENTS:

This book is written for teens, but we didn't want to leave out information for Mom and Dad, too. See our special section, starting on page 227, just for parents.

Chapter 1

THE NEWS

By now (since you're reading this guide), your parents have shared the news. Most likely, the minute you found out marked a dividing line in your life.

> "A parent's cancer is a curveball life throws at you—and it hits you in the face."
>
> —Marlene of Washington, whose dad was diagnosed with cancer when she was fourteen. She cried for ten minutes nonstop when her parents told her the news.

> "You are not alone. So many of us have gone through similar experiences. The knowledge that other people have felt the same emotions, some of which might seem embarrassing or shameful, is quite liberating."
>
> —Brett N. of California, whose dad died of cancer when he was seven months old and whose mother was diagnosed with breast cancer when he was fourteen

Before cancer: You were a typical teenager.

After the cancer news: Everything seems different. Your parent is facing a serious illness and some combination of not-so-pleasant treatments to fight the disease. You're not too sure when all this will end. Yes, everything is different.

Your parent may change; family routines may change; and you might change, too.

But ultimately, in spite of how different everything feels, you're still you. "Underneath it all," says Marlene, "you're still that person you were before your parent was afflicted."

> "What do I wish I had known when I first found out my mom had cancer? I wish someone had told me that not everyone dies of cancer."
>
> —Fifteen-year-old girl in a support group
> for kids coping with a parent's cancer

1.1 A Hunch

Before your parents officially broke the news to you, you may have noticed something was up. Maybe Mom and Dad were acting weird. (That is, weirder than usual.) Maybe you came across an email, overheard a phone call with a doctor, or just listened in on your parents talking one night.

Or maybe you were totally oblivious.

Words of Wisdom:
"When a parent gets sick, it's like the rug of the universe has been pulled out from under your feet. The sense of naïve innocence that all is right in the world falls apart."

—Social worker Bunty Anderson

Marc says: Marsha and I kept the news of her diagnosis from the kids over the three-day weekend before school started. We didn't want to add to the stress of starting a new school year. But it was hell on us. Marsha was depressed and worried. At one point, Maya and her sister, Daniela, were doing something to push all her buttons in that special way teenagers can. And Marsha just snapped at them, "You can't imagine how I feel right now."

Maya says: I just thought it was Mom in a bad mood.

2

"They found out right before Christmas, so my mom kept it a secret from us over the holidays because they didn't want to ruin the holidays."

—Cayla of Colorado, whose father was diagnosed
with colon cancer when she was twelve

Or you might be well aware that something is going on. Liahona of Utah knew her mother had been making lots of doctor's appointments. And then, after a few weeks, she found out why: cancer. "It wasn't like a humongous shock," says the fourteen-year-old. "Because I was in on the step-by-step, I knew kind of what was happening."

Survival Tip: Good communication is a two-way street. If it bothered you that your parents didn't tell you right away, tell them so. In the future they'll at least be aware that you want to find things out when they do.

Stephanie's Story: The Last to Know

Stephanie of Utah, who's fourteen, found out in a not-so-ideal way. When she was a seventh grader, her mom was her soccer coach. One day at practice, a friend came up to Stephanie and said, "Oh, I'm so sorry!" Stephanie was confused and asked what had happened. "Oh, about the cancer," her friend replied. Stephanie's mom had told all of her teammates on the soccer team that she had been diagnosed with cancer but hadn't revealed the news to Stephanie yet. "Boy, that made me feel special," she recalled. "I was pretty mad. It was embarrassing."

In some families, the news may not be a first-time cancer diagnosis but a return of cancer after a couple of years. One girl recalls how she grew up knowing that her mother had had a mastectomy before she was even born and accepted it "just like a part of our life."

When this girl was thirteen, her mom was diagnosed with a recurrence of breast cancer. To her, "it just seemed like something that was traumatic but not a killer." She stayed calm: "I never thought my mom was going to die. It was more like, 'Oh crap, she's got cancer again.'"

1.2 Why Your Parents Told You the Way They Did

Maybe they told you at a family meeting, if that's your family's style. Or maybe they told you in the car.

Marc says: My wife and I picked up Maya and Daniela from school and told them that Marsha had breast cancer. It was easier to tell them in the car than at home. We didn't have to summon them to the kitchen table. We could just kind of say it. And we didn't have to look them in the eye. So…less tension, for us at least.

Maya says: The car was a good place to be told because no one could stomp off to her room or disperse for at least thirty minutes after we found out.

Gia, who's now twenty and lives in Baltimore, found out by text. She knew her mom was going in for biopsy results. The text message worked well for her. Gia says it gave her time to think about what the news meant before she actually talked to her mom.

Carol, who was a freshman in college when her mother was diagnosed with cancer, didn't find out until after her mom had surgery. "I was angry that my parents didn't tell me until after my mom's surgery," she recalls. "They didn't want me to worry or skip my finals to come home. It took me a long time to understand how and why they made that decision."

1.2.1 SUGARCOATING

Some parents may try to "sugarcoat" the moment by coupling the bad news with a dose of fun. Sounds a little nutty, but...why not?

"They told us about it and we started freaking out a little. To cheer everyone up, we just started to play a bunch of games," recalls Tyler T., fourteen, of Utah, whose mom was diagnosed with breast cancer when he was in the fifth grade. Engaging in a regular activity as a family—especially something fun—right after you find out can help keep things normal and remind everyone that life goes on. You can still have fun as a family in spite of cancer.

Perfectly Normal: Don't feel guilty for having fun, laughing, smiling, or going out. Life beats on in spite of bad news. Good cheer can help you and your family cope.

> "They took me to Barnes & Noble and bought me a stuffed-animal deer and we sat down at Starbucks and they gave me cheesecake and they told me."
>
> —Allison B., thirteen, of Idaho

Survival Tip: Let the good times roll. Even if you're not up for fun when you find out, don't think that the cancer months will be devoid of anything fun. Don't be afraid to suggest or plan short family trips if your parent with cancer is up for it, or a family game night or a movie night. Or a hike if you're an outdoorsy family. Getting out of the house during the months of treatment is a good way to break out of the tough routine of cancer treatment.

1.2.2 Tears Might Be Shed

Be prepared. You may never have seen parental tears before. But *cancer* is a scary word, and it can trigger deep emotions.

"After he told us, we kinda talked it out," says Austen, fifteen, of Utah, whose father was diagnosed with leukemia when Austen was ten. "My sister and brother started crying. And that was the first time I've ever seen my dad cry."

Cancer might make you think about death, about the possibility of losing a parent. Maybe a parent you love very much. Maybe a parent you're mad at...but still...it's your parent. The specter of death is a heavy load for anyone, and it's definitely not something that teens tend to think about. Until the word "cancer" arrives at your front door.

Try to get the best information you can from your parents about the prognosis, the word doctors use to describe the outcome they expect. In other words: how tough a fight is ahead, and what are the odds that your parent will survive? If the prognosis is good, that's a relief. If there's concern, then that's not a relief, but it doesn't mean there's no hope. In Chapter 12, we talk about coping with a dire prognosis.

1.2.3 Harsh Words Might Be Spoken

You wouldn't be alone if your first reaction to the cancer news is something like, "Does this mean you can't take me for my driver's license next week?" Or: "How are we going to go shopping for my prom dress?"

. . . .

Abby's Story: She Had to Go to the Movies
It was about three o'clock in the afternoon. Abby
O'Leary's mom told her daughter the news: she had
cancer. Abby had plans to go to a movie that night
with twelve of her friends. The movie was *She's All
That*. Here's what was in Abby's head: "There was big
anticipation about this movie. For weeks, it was all we
could talk about. I wanted to go see this movie. I wasn't
going to cancel my plans." She remembers: "I freaked
out. I ran a mile through the neighborhood" to a best
friend's house.

Her friend's mom persuaded her to call home and
report her whereabouts. But Abby didn't let the cancer
news interfere with her plans. She went to the movie,
which was about a girl whose mother dies of cancer.
"It was not great timing," Abby remembers. In general,
she says, "I was pretty pissed that my mom had been
diagnosed with cancer. I was thirteen, ready to go to
high school. One thing that stuck out was me wanting to make sure I could get rides to do things with
my friends."

. . . .

That kind of reaction doesn't make you a horrible person.
Child life specialist Kathleen McCue, who directs children's
programs at The Gathering Place, a cancer support group in
Cleveland, explains that teens are at a natural stage in life
where they focus on themselves. So it's okay if you had that
reaction. "Blame it on your developmental stage," says McCue.
"What's most important to you is what you want, what you
need, what you're excited about, what you're frightened of."

If you do feel bad about your reaction, you can do the hardest thing in the world for a teenager to do: apologize to your

parents. You can say, "I'm sorry. It's not that I don't love you. I feel bad about what I said."

1.2.4 Honesty: The Best Policy

Are they telling me everything? Do I want to know everything? These are questions that come up at the start, when your parents first tell you…and keep coming up as treatment goes on.

> "I didn't believe my mom and aunt were being honest when they said everything was okay."
>
> —John of New Jersey, whose mom was diagnosed with breast cancer when he was fourteen and a freshman in high school

"Different strokes for different folks" is a cliché you might have heard. Like most clichés, it's got a lot of truth to it.

Different parents have different styles. So do different teenagers. Maybe you don't really want to know the whole story. And you don't have to know every little detail. Or maybe you crave lots of data.

Jake, of Massachusetts, asked his parents to tell him everything about his mom's ovarian cancer. And they did. "I was really grateful for that," says Jake, who was eleven at the time of diagnosis and is now thirteen. "[It] prepared me for what was going to happen."

Words of Wisdom:
"My children have told me over the years the thing that helped them most was that I was always honest. They never worried: is there something else going on, is she telling me the whole story?"

—Wendy Harpham, a physician who was diagnosed with lymphoma in 1990 and has had seven recurrences. Her three children are now in their twenties.

If you feel like your parents have withheld any information, you may want to come up with a list of questions to ask them. Chapter 3 will talk about the different ways your family can keep communication going even at a very stressful time.

(MOM AND) POP QUIZ:

Not sure where to start the conversation?

Here are some questions you may want to ask your parents.

- What kind of cancer is it?
- What kind of treatment will you have?
- Do the doctors think the treatments have a good chance of success?
- What kind of symptoms and side effects will you have from the cancer and the treatments?
- What will change for me?
- What can I do for you?

Joe's mom has a cancer that's tough to treat. Channing's mom has a cancer that usually responds well to treatment. But Joe is handling the news better than Channing.

Wait...that makes no sense! Or does it?

The reason that Joe is doing better than Channing can be found in a study from the *Scandinavian Journal of Psychology*. The study followed fifty-four adolescents who had a parent with cancer. If the outlook for the parent is good, the study reported, the parents might not pay as much attention to the kids. So even though things aren't too bad, the parents aren't telling their children a lot about the cancer and aren't asking the kids, "How are you doing?" That lack of communication can create a lot of teen worries.

On the other hand, if the outlook is not so good, the parents might pay more attention to how their teens are doing. And that kind of attention is incredibly helpful.

Another study, looking at nearly 300 adolescents and published in *Supportive Care in Cancer*, had a similar conclusion. Lead author Stacey Donofrio and others wrote, "Adolescents may feel especially uncertain about their parent's cancer if they feel their parents are not being entirely open."

If your parents aren't giving you the information you need, you can impress them with your knowledge of cancer studies (and maybe get them to open up) by quoting Dr. Donofrio.

1.2.5 THE BURDEN OF UNKNOWNS

For all of you out there taking algebra, you know what it's like to have an unknown in the equation. Think about your parent's cancer as if it's an algebra equation with different variables. Some of the variables (say, x and y) might be easy to figure out. But z might still be a mystery.

> "I was really confused. It was kind of frustrating that she didn't have all the answers. She reassured us as soon as she found out something she would tell us. She didn't want to tell us stuff she didn't know for sure."
>
> —Paul of Maryland, fifteen, whose mom was treated for breast cancer and is now doing well

So even if your parents are really open, there will still be some unknowns. Over time, as your parent visits with doctors and learns more about the diagnosis and treatments, many of your questions will be answered. But not all of them. Unknowns may be something you'll have to accept when dealing with your parent's cancer.

Tyler R.'s parents told him everything after his dad, Chuck, was diagnosed with lymphoma. Tyler was eleven at the time. His mom and dad said: "We don't know where it's going to go or what's going to happen. But we are going to fight it and take it one day and treatment at a time."

The treatments took a toll. "There were days when I thought I was ready to take my last breath," Chuck remembers. He was scared. Tyler was, too. But they made it through all the unknowns, and Chuck is today in good health.

1.3 Why You Reacted the Way You Did

Probably you were a little bit shocked. And maybe angry. And depressed.

You have a lot of company in the world of teenagers.

Research has shown that teenagers are often more affected by a parent's cancer diagnosis than younger children. In several studies of children facing a parent's cancer diagnosis, researchers found the teens more likely to show signs of depression and anxiety. And the reason is…your teenagerness.

teen*age*er*ness (noun): The state of being on the road to independence and trying to find out what that means.

And now you're on another road. And it may involve a lot of household responsibilities, which typically fall to the older children in a family where a parent has cancer. "Adolescents have been found to feel torn between the normative tasks of their age groups (forming relationships outside the family) and the need to deal with the practical, psychological, and social tasks demanded by the illness," wrote family therapy professor Maureen Davey and other researchers in a study published in the *Journal of Marital and Family Therapy*.

In other words, not only does cancer suck, but being a teenager who has a parent with cancer sucks, too, and maybe even more than it does for your younger siblings.

But there are ways to deal with the stress. We'll get to that topic in Chapter 6.

1.4 A Charged Word

As soon as you find out your parent has cancer, the word might start to take on a personality of its own. When you hear the word—whether it's uttered by your parents, a friend, or on

TV—it might spark feelings of anxiety, depression, or fear. It might even give you chills down your spine.

"Just hearing the word makes me feel uncomfortable," says Jake of Massachusetts, whose mother was diagnosed with ovarian cancer. "If I'm out with friends and they say cancer or say something about people with cancer—anything really—I kind of like clam up. I'm usually very talkative."

Survival Tip: *It's Just a Word!* Don't let the word "cancer" make you upset. Say it over and over again until the word loses its meaning. Write the word on a piece of paper and tear it up into a million pieces. Tell the word "cancer" who's boss!

The Greek physician Hippocrates gets the dubious credit for inventing the word "cancer." Hippocrates, (aka the Father of Medicine) used the Greek word for crab, *carcinos*, to describe a tumor. Think about the similarities between a crab and a cancer tumor: they both have finger-like spreading projections. A few hundred years later, Celsus, a Roman physician, translated the Greek term *carcinos* into the Latin word *cancer*.

Perfectly Normal: Does the word "cancer" freak you out? Don't worry, that happens to a lot of kids. "I immediately have an emotional internal reaction to talking about it. It brings me back to my dad every time." —Cayla of Colorado, whose father faced colon cancer when she was twelve and is today in good health

Chapter 2

CANCER 101

"Know yourself, know your enemy"
— Ancient Chinese proverb quoted in *The Art of War*

What is cancer, anyway?
You've surely heard of it, but you may not know much about it.
Now (all of a sudden) it's invading your life!
It's up to you how much you choose to learn about the disease that has affected one of your parents. It may be helpful to know at least the basics so you understand what's going on.

> "I want to know the science behind everything. It was interesting to me. The feeling of being more aware helped me. I like to know things. When there's less doubt in a situation, even if it's bad, you can accept it."
>
> —John of New Jersey, whose mother was diagnosed with breast cancer when he was a freshman in high school

"Get into it," recommends Ryan Urich, whose father, actor Robert Urich, was diagnosed with cancer while Ryan was in college. "Know what you're dealing with. It can be this horrible suffocating dark cloud that hangs over your family and chokes every breath out of you. But know what you're up against, know what fight you're gonna be making. Even if you're not the person with the diagnosis, you're going to be right there with the person with the diagnosis. You can't ignore it; it's not going to go away. Until cancer is like polio and every person has a vaccination, know what you're up against." Ryan has completed medical school and is now a resident in internal medicine. His father's illness was not a "motivator" in his career path, he says, then adds, "The subconscious is a hell of a thing. Maybe a tiny part of me is trying to understand what my father went through."

If you're interested in starting your crash course in cancer, read through this chapter. If you have more questions, refer to our Resources section at the end of this book. And if you'd rather not know much and instead want to focus on being there for your parent, skip ahead to Chapter 3.

First things first: what do you know about cancer to start? You may know just the basics (that it's a serious disease) or you may have learned more in a science class.

• •

What did you know about cancer when your parent was diagnosed?

- Kaitlin: "I thought it was like the flu."

- Paul: "I really didn't know what cancer actually was. I heard about it from TV. I knew it was bad. Those were the biggest questions: what was it, and how do you get rid of it?"

- Jake: "We studied it in school that year, so I knew it was a cluster of cells. My mom's grandfather and father were diagnosed so I knew that it could be deadly. I would never have guessed that it would happen to my mom."

- Jenny: "I took AP biology in high school so I learned about it. It's different when it's happening in your mother's body."

• •

Head Count: We surveyed 53 teens coping with a parent's cancer and adults who were teenagers when their parent was diagnosed. Here's what they knew at the outset:

- 39% said "just the basics"

- 30% said "as much as I needed to"

- 26% said "next to nothing"

- 5% said "knew a lot"

2.1 THE BIG QUESTION MARKS

We collected questions from teens coping with a parent's cancer, and we posed those questions to a team of experts. Our main advisers were:

- **Anna Franklin, MD**, assistant professor in the Department of Pediatrics at the Children's Cancer Hospital of the University of Texas MD Anderson Cancer Center.
- **Mary Hardy, MD**, medical director of the Simms/Mann-UCLA Integrative Oncology Program. (In case you're wondering, integrative medicine combines conventional treatments with what are called "complementary" treatments—herbs, aromatherapy, and stress-reducing practices like yoga and meditation.)
- **Lidia Schapira, MD**, assistant professor of medicine at Harvard Medical School.
- **Eliezer M. Van Allen, MD**, a Fellow in Medical Oncology at Dana-Farber/Partners Cancer Care and a post-doctoral fellow in the lab of Levi Garraway. He cofounded the UCLA branch of Camp Kesem, which serves children who have had a parent with cancer.

These doctors are oncologists—that's the term for a doctor who specializes in the treatment of cancer. (From the Greek "onco," meaning tumor, and "ology," meaning study of.)

These doctors gave us lots of answers. They also pointed out that some questions have several different answers. And the answer may start with "it depends…" In addition, some questions about cancer have no answers at this time. That's frustrating for patients and their family members…and for doctors, too.

So, what is cancer anyway?

Before we answer that question, a word about cells. Your body is made up of about 10 trillion cells, give or take a few. There are different types of cells, and they have different functions. They are what make up your bones, your blood, your organs, and *you*!

It's normal for cells to grow. Cells grow by dividing. When you're young, cells grow more quickly to allow you to grow. When you're older, cells no longer grow as quickly and only divide to replace old, damaged, or dying cells.

FYI: Much of the time, this group of growing cancer cells forms a tumor, but cancer cells can also form in the blood or in bone marrow (the spongy tissue in the center of most bones that makes red blood cells) or in the body's lymphatic system (which carries fluids through the body).

Dr. Franklin: "Cancer occurs when a group of cells in a certain part of the body grows abnormally and uncontrollably. There are many different kinds of cancer based on where the cancer starts."

Dr. Schapira: "The cancers can be very different depending on where they are in the body. They can be very small or large."

Dr. Hardy: "Generally, the tumor itself is less of a problem than where the cancer decides to grow."

Do we know why cancer cells start growing in the first place?

Dr. Van Allen: "Cancer cells have acquired changes in their DNA that make them work a different way. They start to divide rapidly and uncontrollably. The cells that surround these damaged cells should send a signal that says 'stop growing.' But cancer cells keep going. So the damaged cells keep on making new cells, all of them with damaged DNA."

FYI: Those cells can grow in lots of places. Cancer is really an umbrella term for more than one hundred diseases of this type. For example, cancer can grow in the breast or in the lungs. There's cancer of the blood (leukemia) and cancer of the bone (osteosarcoma). All the different types of cancer are caused by uncontrolled cell growth.

Why is DNA sending the wrong signal?

There isn't a great answer to this question. The possibilities are that a) your parent inherited a cancerous gene (that accounts for about 10 percent of cancer cases), or b) your parent was exposed to something in the environment that caused them to get cancer, or c) it's totally random. Why does that random mistake happen in some people and not others? That's still a mystery.

Dr. Van Allen: A lot of research is focused on trying to understand why cancer happens. And then we can better understand what to do about it.

What does it mean if a cancer is Stage 1, 2, 3, or 4?

Like most things in life, cancer is not black and white. There are many shades of cancer. It can be really serious or easily taken care of. It can show up in your lungs or on your skin. It can be removed by a small surgery or require a long period of treatment.

Dr. Schapira: "Staging refers to the extent of cancer. Doctors determine this by running tests, such as CAT scans, MRIs, and bone scans. This allows them to figure out if the cancer has spread to other parts of the body and to assign a number. Stage 1 means the cancer is limited to the organ where it started and Stage 4 means the cancer has spread to other organs. Stages 2 and 3 typically mean there is some spread to lymph nodes in the vicinity of the original cancer."

FYI: A CT scan or CAT scan is short for computed tomography, a sophisticated combination of X-ray images. Whoa, that sounds complicated! But it's really just a way to take pictures of shapes inside your body to find cancer. Some cancers began exhibiting symptoms fairly quickly. Others can go unnoticed and without symptoms for a long time.

Dr. Franklin: "A lower stage means the cancer is localized in one part of the body and can be easier to treat. Stage 4 typically means that the cancer has spread to places far away from the original site of the tumor." And that makes it harder to treat.

Each type of cancer may have special characteristics that go into assigning it a stage, and not every cancer is staged the same way.

The National Cancer Institute has a thorough explanation of the different ways to stage different cancers at its website, cancer.gov

How can you have cancer and not know it until a doctor runs a test?

Dr. Schapira: "Some cancers hide in places in the body that are too deep to feel. If the cancerous cells are not touching or pressing on any vital organ, there may not be any symptoms until the cancer is quite large. Or you may have cancer in the blood and not know it until you feel very rundown and tired. Then the doctor most likely will notice you're pale and thin and order a blood test."

Dr. Franklin: "You're going to feel a lymph node in your armpit much earlier than something that's inside your abdomen. If you've got a melanoma on your skin, you're going to see that much earlier than something inside your body."

How long has the cancer been there?

Dr. Franklin: "There's no way to know, really, unless the person had a CT scan six months ago and nothing was there and then had a CT scan for another reason and now something's there."

Diagnosis vs. prognosis: what's the difference?

Dr. Schapira: "A *diagnosis* means an expert puts everything together and comes up with an answer to the problem. For there to be a diagnosis of cancer, in almost all circumstances there needs to be a sampling of cancer, or a biopsy, where a piece of cancer is retrieved by inserting a small needle through the skin or sometimes by a more extensive surgical operation or blood test or sampling of bone marrow.

"*Prognosis* refers to the likely outcome for somebody who has this, what's likely going to happen. Like a weather forecast, a prognosis is based on certain elements.

"Doctors take samples of the cancer, run blood tests, and take X-rays to determine exactly what type of cancer it is, how large it has grown, and whether it has spread to other areas of the body. The prognosis is based on the doctor's knowledge of the disease and an understanding of the patient's situation."

Cancer Vocab: Metastasis. That's the medical term for "spread," as in cancer cells have spread from their place of origin—say, the breast—to other parts of the body. The word's roots are Greek. "Meta" means "next" and "stasis" means "placement." When cancer cells travel to other parts of the body, where they grow and build new tumors, that is called metastasis. The cancer has metastasized. The patient has metastatic disease.

Whether your parent will be successfully treated for cancer depends on what the doctors find out.

Dr. Schapira: "The doctor might say that with a certain kind of treatment, the person is going to be fine and live out a normal life. Or maybe there's a 50/50 chance of treatment being successful. Some cancers often respond well to treatment—breast cancer, for example. Some are difficult to treat, like pancreatic cancer. Your parent's overall health can also be important in determining how well they do. After the information is gathered and the doctor makes sense of it, the doctor can give your parent a prognosis.

"The prognosis is not always right (like weather forecasts). But it does convey what's likely to happen."

Dr. Hardy: "The thing about the prognosis that I think is really important is that it doesn't define the outcome for any particular person. Stating the average prognosis as if it's the absolute truth is psychologically devastating. If a prognosis is not good and you tell a patient they have two weeks to live, some people will follow that direction. My stance is to say, 'We know this is serious. We're doing everything possible. Don't worry about numbers. Do the best you can for yourself.' That way, the patient shows us what's going to happen."

Are all cancers pretty much the same?

Cancers all share certain characteristics, like uncontrolled cell growth. What's not the same is the way the cancer behaves, how it grows, how fast it grows, and so on. Also, different types of cancer are treated with different procedures.

Dr. Schapira: "There are hundreds of different kinds of cancers. What they have in common is that the body doesn't need the cells, but once they start growing, the body can't regulate their growth."

If my dad has prostate cancer but it spread to his kidneys, is it still called prostate cancer?

The type of cancer your parent has is identified by the part of the body where the cancer started growing. So, yes it would still be called prostate cancer.

Am I at risk because my parent has cancer?

Dr. Schapira: "The answer to that is maybe. It depends on the kind of cancer and whether or not it's a cancer linked to genes."

And what should I do if I am at risk?

Dr. Schapira: "Even if there is a family history of cancer, that doesn't mean it's going to happen to you. It's very rare for teens to be immediately at risk. A good message is to do everything you can to be healthy. That's about all you can do."

• •

If Mom Has Breast Cancer, Will I Get It, Too?

Mom has breast cancer. A daughter may feel that's going to be her fate as well. Or maybe she thinks she already has the disease. The website breastcancer.org surveyed 2,500 girls ages eight to eighteen and found that almost a third believe they currently have breast cancer.

Perhaps the preteen or teen is mistaking a sign of breast development—a seeming lump on one side as the breasts develop, for example—as a sign of breast cancer. But the fact is that "breast cancer is extremely rare in girls," says oncologist Marisa Weiss, founder of breastcancer.org. Sure, you may have seen or read a story about a teenager with breast cancer. "The media is going to play up that story to get attention," says Weiss. "But it's not representative or normal."

Nor does a parent's diagnosis automatically mean the child is fated to develop the disease. Only 1 in 10 cases of breast cancer are "due to one of the inherited genes you hear about," Weiss says. A genetic counselor can talk with your mom about the advisability of testing for the so-called BRCA, or breast cancer, genes.

For any daughter of a breast cancer patient, the standard mammogram guidelines apply: yearly mammograms starting at age forty. But screening may need to start earlier if the patient was diagnosed with premenopausal breast cancer. In such situations, it's important to start mammograms ten years prior to the age of the youngest affected relative. If your mother was diagnosed at age forty, that means you should start being screened at age thirty.

But you don't just have to wait and see. "Take steps to be as healthy as possible," advises Weiss, whose website offers advice as does her book, *Taking Care of Your "Girls": A Breast Health Guide for Girls, Teens, and In-Betweens*. Studies have shown that three alcoholic drinks a week raise your risk 15 percent compared to nondrinkers. Smoking and being overweight also increase the risk. Four to seven hours of moderate to intense exercise a week results in a lower risk.

• •

Did I cause the cancer in some way? Is my mom or dad responsible for causing the cancer? Was it preventable?

You did *nothing* to cause the cancer. You should never feel guilty about your parent's cancer because it's not your fault, not even a little bit.

And in any case, looking back doesn't get you anywhere. Dr. Franklin recommends concentrating on the fact that doctors are treating your parent's cancer. "That's where we need to put our energy, rather than worrying about what you did in the past that could have caused it," advises Dr. Franklin.

What are the chances of survival?

Some cancers are easier to treat than others. Some are easily treated; others are untreatable. The stage of your parent's cancer will give you some idea of the prospects.

Dr. Hardy: "Just like every pneumonia doesn't kill you, neither will every cancer kill you. Response rates are quite good. It's a nasty fight but it's a winnable fight."

Some cancers are 100 percent curative, meaning there is a 100 percent chance of survival.

Dr. Schapira: "If you have a cancer of the bowel caught at very early stage or cancer of uterus at very early stage, surgery alone is what we call curative, associated with a 100 percent chance of survival."

2.2 Treatments and Their Side Effects

While there isn't a quick cure for cancer, doctors can use effective treatments to make someone's cancer go away. But many of the treatments for cancer will make your parent sick. It seems strange that something meant to make someone better in the long run will make them seem worse in the short term. Many of the telltale signs of someone battling cancer — weakness, weight loss, hair loss — are actually side effects of chemotherapy. And side effects vary. Some patients do just fine while on chemo; others, not so much. Ditto for radiation.

Dr. Schapira: "These treatments are the tools we have to fight cancer. We don't always use all of them. How much we use of one treatment or another depends on the individual case or circumstances, the kind of tumor, and how far the cancer has spread."

"Expect the unexpected. What happens, happens, you know. Sometimes treatments work. Sometimes they don't."
—Lance, fourteen, of Virginia, whose mom is battling metastatic breast cancer

SURGERY

Dr. Franklin: "Surgery basically is removing a tumor. Some cancers are treated with surgery, some are treated with chemotherapy, some just with radiation, and some with a combination of two or three of those. The order of treatment depends on the size and nature of the tumor. With certain cancers, if you take out the big tumor, chemotherapy and radiation can be more effective and don't have to do as much work, don't have to kill as many cells. With some cancers, doctors will do what they call neo-adjuvant chemotherapy. The patient gets some chemo after diagnosis, then chemotherapy shrinks the tumor a bit. That makes the surgery a little easier."

FYI: Depending on the nature of the surgery, your mom or dad may have to spend some days in the hospital and will recuperate further at home, regaining strength. Surgery takes a lot out of someone! But once it's over, there's usually forward movement toward recovery. That's not necessarily the case for chemotherapy.

"I always made my dad silly beaded yarn bracelets and a necklace to go into surgery. Doctors make you take off your jewelry, but he made the doctors let him keep the bracelet on his wrist for good luck."
—Cayla of Colorado, whose father survived colon cancer

CHEMOTHERAPY

Chemotherapy is when doctors insert chemicals into the body that will kill off cancer cells. The chemicals can be taken orally as a pill or intravenously (IV) into a vein in the arm or other part of the body. If the patient has small veins, the doctor may surgically implant a port to deliver the drugs. Drugs may even be injected into spinal fluid in some cases.

The doctors estimate how many chemicals will be needed, but they aren't going to give the total amount to your parent all at once. That would be too many chemicals for the body to handle. Instead, they break up the dosage into rounds given at intervals—maybe something like six doses spread out over six months.

Dr. Franklin: "Chemotherapy is a fancy word for medicines to treat cancer. Chemotherapy kills cancer cells but it also kills normal cells, so your body does have to spend a lot of time healing the damage to the normal cells. It is something toxic, and we have this center in our brain that makes us recognize when something toxic is in our system, and that can cause nausea and vomiting. And because it damages normal cells as well, chemotherapy can have the side effect of dropping your red blood cell counts and decreasing your energy."

The problem is that conventional chemotherapy isn't targeted to attack just cancer cells. The chemo chemicals affect the whole body, causing an array of negative side effects. The good news is that most of the side effects are temporary. And many newer drugs target the cancer cells while bringing on fewer side effects.

Dr. Schapira: "You might have a parent who is absolutely well, and the treatment makes them feel weak and sick, makes them lose their hair, their appetite. That's because chemotherapy drugs affect the entire body; they don't just target the cancer. You can use the expression 'collateral damage' to explain that some normal cells are also damaged, albeit temporarily.

"The goal for all cancer is to find what we call targeted, or personalized, treatment that will cause little collateral damage but will prevent the cancer from growing so over time it basically disappears."

Almost every chemotherapy drug affects bone marrow and the red blood cells, which are responsible for carrying oxygen through the body. So it's common for someone with cancer to feel weaker and sleepy more often than before. Many drugs can also damage the nerve endings and cause discomfort.

Dr. Schapira: "Another thing that happens is that you often don't sleep well, or maybe you're napping more during the day and interrupting your [sleep] rhythms. You're more likely to be irritable. Imagine the combination of not feeling as strong and not looking as well [as you used to]."

Some cancers are highly responsive to chemotherapy and only require a few treatments. Others might need really high doses of chemotherapy to be effective. Some cancers aren't responsive to chemotherapy at all.

Dr. Franklin: "Cancer cells that grow quickly are more responsive to chemotherapy. Chemotherapy works when cells are in the process of dividing, of making two cells out of one cell. A lot of the conventional chemotherapy drugs kill cells by interfering with the DNA copying itself when the cells are dividing. That's why one of the main side effects of chemotherapy is losing hair. Your hair is always growing.

"Chemotherapy doesn't work as well when cancer cells are growing very slowly, like prostate cancer. There's not a chance for these drugs to get in and kill the cells. But there are new targeted therapies that work on cells in different ways."

Dr. Schapira: "The only way to treat some cancers—like leukemia, a blood cancer—is chemotherapy. You can't cut [the cancer cells] out; they're everywhere. The blood circulates everywhere. And you can't give radiation to the blood—it's too toxic."

If chemotherapy works, then the cancer cells are knocked out. Dr. Schapira explains, "The body has more of the good cells so they can keep growing back. It's mathematics." And when those healthy cells do come back, hair will start growing again, for example.

Some cancer patients decide they don't want chemotherapy. The doctor may feel that chemo would not offer much chance of prolonging the patient's life and that the chemo drugs would make life rather unpleasant. The patient may prefer to live their final months without suffering the negative side effects of chemo. See Chapter 12 for more information on a dire prognosis.

RADIATION

Dr. Franklin: "Radiation is focusing an X-ray beam directly on the tumor and having that beam killing the cancer cells."

About half of cancer patients are radiated. A machine delivers the dose.

Radiation does not make a patient radioactive. But it can cause side effects. As with chemotherapy, the side effects vary from patient to patient. Some of the impact is similar to what chemo can cause: fatigue, nausea (if the abdomen is targeted), and hair loss (if the head or neck is targeted).

Then there are the side effects that are not at all like those from chemo: skin irritation and the development of scar tissue that can inhibit movement in the affected area.

BONE MARROW TRANSPLANT

It sounds like a big deal. And it is. The patient is hospitalized, and, through an IV, doctors infuse marrow into the vein. A bone marrow transplant is performed after high doses of chemotherapy to wipe out the cancer. The chemo wipes out marrow as well.

Dr. Schapira: "For patients with solid tumors, a bone

marrow transplant usually means all other treatments haven't worked and it's a desperate thing. But for leukemias and blood cancers, it's a way to deliver high doses of chemotherapy and there's a good chance of being cured."

COMPLEMENTARY TREATMENTS

There's traditional medicine that a doctor will prescribe for cancer: surgery, chemotherapy, radiation. And then there are complementary treatments that a doctor might recommend or that your parent might decide to try. These treatments aren't intended to replace the standard tactics but to complement them—to be used along with them in the hope of providing additional benefits for the patient.

There is evidence that acupuncture and yoga, for example, can reduce some of the side effects caused by chemotherapy, like fatigue and nausea. But there is no evidence that any complementary treatments can cure cancer.

Dr. Schapira: "There are lots of complementary treatments that can help preserve quality of life. The ones I think are most helpful are the ones that deal with power of the mind. Meditation, for instance. Anything that can harness the power of the mind to soothe or promote peace."

WHY DOES CANCER SOMETIMES COME BACK?

That's a tough question. The hope is always that after treatment, the patient will be done with cancer. But some cancers come back. Cancer cells can be very aggressive, and some do not respond to treatment. So cancer can recur—sometimes in the same place where it began, sometimes in a part of the body that's distant from the original site. When cancer comes back, treatment comes back as well. But recurrence can be more difficult to treat successfully.

Dr. Hardy: "In dodgeball, the slowest kids are picked off first. When you get down to a smaller number of kids, they're faster and harder to hit. It's just like that for chemo. Sometimes the cells that don't get killed off early are the most resistant, the ones that grow back."

2.3 The Cure: Why Isn't There One Yet?

If cancer has been around for so long, why isn't there a cure yet? One answer is that cancer is a tough nut to crack.

Dr. Franklin: "There are some things about some cancers that we understand very well, but other things that we don't understand as well."

Does the money that goes to cancer research really help?

Researchers are working hard to understand the mysteries of cancer. And they get a lot of their funding from cancer organizations.

Dr. Franklin: "What those organizations do is end up giving that money to researchers to help them understand cancer. Every research study doesn't always come out with the planned results, but it's sort of like when Thomas Edison was inventing the lightbulb. How many things did he go through before he figured out exactly how to make it work?"

What are researchers doing now to come up with better treatments?

Dr. Schapira: "A good analogy to say is that we're trying to locate the light switches inside these cancer cells and figure out a way to turn them off, to inactivate those cells. The dream is to be able to do that for every cancer."

Turning off those switches would be the job of "designer drugs" researchers are working on that are "designed to target" a cancer cell. "Almost every day some progress is made," Dr. Schapira says.

We know a lot about cancer. But we don't always know how a patient will react to treatment. And sometimes the patient does far better than anyone could have imagined.

Dr. Hardy: "Anyone can get surprised [by a patient's positive reaction to treatment]. I love it; I think it's excellent; I like being surprised. I think that's a triumph of mind and spirit over matter, and to me that's exciting, so I welcome it. People will attribute survival to all kinds of things. Even if I don't agree with them, I welcome it. I think it's great."

2.4 True or False

Cancer was around during Cleopatra's time.

True. You hear a lot about cancer today but it's not a new thing. It's been around for as long as we (or anyone) can remember. Scientists have even found evidence of cancer in Egyptian mummies and references to the disease in manuscripts written around 3000 BC. At that time, the manuscript noted, "There is no treatment." Today, we're fortunate to have many kinds of effective treatments.

All cancer is hereditary.

False. Actually, only 5 to 10 percent of cancers are hereditary.

Cancer is contagious.

False. Cancer is not the common cold. You can't catch it. But there are a couple of things to note. A virus called HPV can transmit cervical cancer through sexual contact. (And there's now a vaccine to protect people from that virus.) Also, if you're around someone who smokes a lot and inhale secondhand smoke, you increase your risk of lung cancer.

Approximately 1.7 million Americans are diagnosed with cancer every year.

True. That represents about half of 1 percent of the United States population.

Deodorant and antiperspirant cause breast cancer.

False. Dr. Eli Van Allen hears that a lot when he speaks to campers at Camp Kesem, a program for children who are coping with a parent's cancer. And campers aren't the only ones who make this connection. It's all over the Internet. Now it is true that doctors check a woman's armpit as part of breast cancer exams. But that's because primary breast cancers spread to the lymph nodes in the underarm area, not the other way around. "There is no evidence that antiperspirants cause breast cancer," Dr. Van Allen says.

Lung cancer is always caused by smoking cigarettes.

False. Smoking causes nine out of ten lung cancer cases in the United States. Other causes: exposure to secondhand smoke or to substances like asbestos, diesel fumes, or radon, a natural gas emitted by rocks and soil that can be trapped in homes or offices. Radon gas is responsible for approximately 20,000 lung cancer cases every year.

Cigarette smoking causes only lung cancer.

False. Cigarette smoking can also cause cancer of the mouth, nose, throat, voice box, esophagus, bladder, kidney, pancreas, cervix, stomach, blood, and bone marrow.

Metastatic disease is harder to treat.

True. Doctors must not only target the primary cancer but also the cancer that's spread to other organs.

Stress causes cancer.

False. "There's a ton of folklore written about that," Dr. Schapira says. "The short answer is no. Some studies link the function of the immune system to stress, but to point the finger and say stress, grief, or overwork causes cancer is really ridiculous and should be discouraged. It may lead to unnecessary guilt, which is a bad emotion. It feeds into the idea that we have more control over our life than we really do."

You will die if you have cancer.

False. According to American Cancer Society statistics, the five-year survival rate for patients diagnosed between 2001 and 2007 is 67 percent, compared to 49 percent for people diagnosed in the mid-1970s. That's progress—not enough progress, but still an encouraging trend.

2.5 Tell Me More!

If you want to seek out more in-depth information about cancer or find answers to more complex or specific questions, tons of resources can help you.

You might be tempted to go online and start googling kinds of cancer. Don't just dive in. You'll come across some frightening facts. And then maybe start freaking out.

Make sure you're seeking out credible resources. A cancer center with ".org" after its name is better than some random ".com" website.

But even if you go to the most credible cancer source on the Internet, you still might not get information that's relevant to your parent's situation. Maybe you'll find out-of-date info or a worst-case scenario.

Dr. Franklin: "I'm reluctant to encourage people to [look up] information on the Internet. Just keep in mind that the information is not specific to any one patient, and it is not always going to be the right information."

Survival Tip: "I'd just say, don't be afraid to ask questions."

—Alison S., whose mom and dad were both diagnosed with cancer—and are doing well today

---

Here are some folks you might approach for more info on cancer:

- **Your parents.** They are getting info from the doctors and probably doing a little research.
- **Relatives or family friends.** Maybe you don't want to bother your parents. Try other folks in your circle, especially anyone who works in the field of medicine.
- **Teachers.** Your biology or genetics teacher should be able to answer basic questions.
- **School nurse.** Another source of information—or referrals to people in the know.
- **Doctors.** Go with your parent to their appointment and ask the doctor the questions you've been saving up.
- **Support groups.** If you belong to any cancer-related support groups (in person or online), bring up things that are confusing you or ask your question. Chances are, someone in the room (or the group facilitator) will know the answer.

For a list of helpful books and websites, see the Resources section at the end of this book.

Chapter 3

LET'S TALK: HOW TO KEEP YOUR FAMILY COMMUNICATION LINES WIDE OPEN

This chapter is about the other "c" word—not cancer, but communication. Communication is hard. It's hard for teens to communicate with their parents. It's hard for parents to communicate with teenage children. And it's especially hard for teens and parents to communicate when Mom or Dad has cancer. Everybody needs help! As the saying goes, communication is a two-way street. So this is a two-way chapter, with advice for both teens and their parents on how to bridge the communication gap. Teens, feel free to highlight the things you want your parents to know. Parents, do the same.

3.1 HOW MUCH DO YOU WANT TO KNOW?

When cancer comes into your family, you may want to know everything you possibly can about it—or as little as possible. More likely, you'll be somewhere in the middle.

So how do you get the info that you need from your parents?

• •

Jackie's Story: "I Want to Know"
Jackie's dad was diagnosed with leukemia. He had some tough treatments and spent some time in the hospital, but then he seemed to be doing well. He was in remission. Things looked promising. Maybe Dad had

beat cancer. Jackie was feeling that life was getting back to normal.

Then one evening the doctor called the family's home phone. Jackie answered. She told her parents to pick up—but she didn't hang up. She listened in. The doctor was talking about the possibility of a bone marrow transplant.

Jackie, who's fourteen, panicked. "Oh my God, it's back," she thought. "My mom hasn't told me." In tears, she ran to a friend's house.

Eventually her parents caught up with her. Her mom explained that her dad was getting a bone marrow transplant to put him in better shape to fight cancer *if* it were to recur.

That's when Jackie laid out her rules: "I made it clear I want to know what's going on. My mother was worried to tell us details; she didn't want us to worry. I told her, 'If there is information you have and you think you shouldn't tell Jackie, that's what I want you to tell me. I want to know as things happen so there's no miscommunication.'"

After that conversation, Jackie says, her mom was a better communicator.

• •

• •

Kaitlin's Story: "I Didn't Want to Know"
Kaitlin's mom was diagnosed with Stage 4 breast cancer. When her mom was in treatment, Kaitlin, who's now fifteen, recalls, "I didn't want to know bad stuff. I'd feel anxious, get nervous." And she sure didn't want to go to any doctor's appointments with her mom: "I'm terrified of needles." Kaitlin liked to retreat to her room, put on her earbuds, and shut out the world.

But Kaitlin's dad didn't leave her alone in her fortress of solitude. Sometimes he'd knock. She'd remove her earbuds. "He'd just tell me how it was," Kaitlin says. "I'd get really upset, but I'm glad he told me." Her dad was straightforward in what he said about her mom's situation. He didn't sugarcoat. That worked for Kaitlin. "I like straightforward information," she says. "You know what to expect."

• •

///

Moral of the Stories:
Chances are, if you tell your parents you want to know everything (or most everything) with no sugarcoating, they'll oblige. So let them know!

///

Even if you prefer the saying "Ignorance is bliss" over the saying "Knowledge is power," you may find that ignorance is not exactly bliss when it comes to your parent's health.

3.2 WHAT IF YOU'RE OUT OF THE LOOP?

Some parents are masters of concealment when it comes to cancer. And hiding the truth can cause a lot of problems.

"The only time I got updates was when it was good news," says Mansoor. His dad was diagnosed with colon cancer when Mansoor was twelve. If there was bad news, his parents wouldn't share it, although Mansoor could figure out something was wrong: "I'd read it through how my parents were acting." They wanted him to have no worries. Sometimes that worked: "I could pretend I was living a normal life." But ultimately, it didn't. He often felt confused. It was kind of a guessing game: *what's up with Dad and his cancer?*

Guessing games might drive you to the Internet for information. And then the floodgates open. You'll find all kinds of information, some of it totally inaccurate. Some of it accurate but not necessarily true for your parent. Some of it outdated. And some of it pretty scary. As we said in Chapter 2, you have to filter what you read on the Internet. The information may be a) not true and b) not relevant to your parent's cancer.

• •

Ryan's Story: The Talk He Wished He'd Had

When his dad, actor Robert Urich, was fighting cancer, Ryan recalls, "I didn't know everything about it. Only in retrospect can I piece together the most probable explanation of what happened." Also, in retrospect, Ryan wishes he had known more at the time. "Know what you're dealing with" is his mantra.

If you're the kind of person who wants to know more and you're not getting the info you crave, Ryan suggests telling your mom or dad: "Hey, look, I'm a part of this. No matter how pretty or ugly it is, whether you like it or not, I am going to be affected by this. Keeping me in the dark is making it worse.

"In hindsight," he adds, "I kinda wish I did sit down and have a talk with my mom and dad."

Keep in Mind: Even when you do get lots of information, that doesn't mean you'll have no questions, worries, or doubts. Alison S., who was fourteen when her mom was diagnosed with breast cancer and whose dad was diagnosed with bladder cancer a few years later, remembers that her parents were pretty open. "I felt like I could ask questions if I wanted to. My biggest memory is just figuring out how to process it."

• •

Ah yes, the processing of information. That's very hard to do. How do you deal with this big change in your household? That's the subject for Chapter 4.

3.3 Reality Check: How Far In the Know Can You Go?
Can you expect to know everything?

> "Your parents will probably not tell you some things. I'm glad they didn't tell us that the oral cancer survival rate is not very good. That would have made it more depressing."
>
> —Dorrie, twelve, whose mother battled oral cancer

Even if you want all the details, and even if you ask a lot of questions, your parents may not be willing to share everything. There may be feelings that are too personal to talk about, or details about treatment that they think would be too upsetting to mention. You have to accept the fact that there may be some things that you are never going to know.

And that may be okay with you.

> "I was a little bit in the loop, but not in terms of how dramatic and painful and horrible the treatments were. I knew my mom was sick and would get nauseous, but I didn't know about the amount of pain. I don't think I would have wanted to know."
>
> —Abby O'Leary, who was thirteen when her mother was diagnosed with cancer

3.4 How to Keep Talking...Even If It's in Writing
Talk with your parents to figure out what kind of communication works best for your family. Some of the options:

⚐ The Family Meeting. If your family has always had family meetings to discuss important stuff, then keep it up. A short family get-together is a chance for parents to update the kids about what's going on with doctor's visits and the like. Figure out how often you want to meet. Once a week or every two weeks might be okay, depending on your parent's treatments. Maybe you could combine family meeting night and pizza night to lighten the mood. Some families create a "Putting Cancer In Its Place" time during the week—say, Sunday dinner, says psychiatrist Karen Weihs.

Keep In Mind: A meet-and-chat is just not the way some families work. What's more, an announcement from Mom and Dad that "Tonight we will have our first family meeting ever in the history of the family" could cause a panic attack. Everyone will think that something must be horribly wrong! If your family hasn't been into meetings before cancer, talk about whether you want to start family meetings during the months of treatment, or whether your parents can find other ways to keep everyone in the loop.

⚐ Regular Updates. Both parents and kids should be flexible. If something important happens in treatment, for good or for bad, the parents might call the family together to catch up. Part of the meeting is what child life specialist Kathleen McCue calls "information passing": *here's what happened at the doctor's. Here's a new treatment plan. Here are some things that have come up about Mom's cancer since the last time we talked.*

You can jot down any questions you have before the family get-together, so you'll remember to ask them.

⚐ Car Talk. Something magical happens when your mom or dad is driving and you're the passenger. You talk about stuff. Maybe that's because you don't have to look at each other. So think of the family ride as a vehicle for more than just transportation. Drives can be an opportunity for the parents or kids to deliver information, ask questions, and just catch up about lots of stuff—from the latest news on how chemo is going to the latest gossip from the halls of the high school.

🎗 **Text and Email.** Sometimes it can be tough to ask questions in person. If your parent is responsive to email or text, don't be afraid to write them a note or let them know that it's ok to text you a quick "thumbs-up" after a doctor appointment.

🎗 **Messages on a Board.** Set up a white board and marker, or some variation, in a corner of the house where everyone hangs out. You can scrawl questions or comments. Mom or Dad can write answers. If you don't want to ask out loud, this might work better for you. You and your parents never even have to be in the same room at the same time—and you're still communicating!

🎗 **Notebook Exchanges.** This is a somewhat less public version of the whiteboard. Keep a notebook or journal on a table in the kitchen, the dining room, or the entry hall. You and your siblings can write anything you want in the notebook. Each day, if possible, Mom or Dad will read the latest entries and respond to your questions and comments.

🎗 **Post-it Notes.** This minimalist approach may be just fine if you're a minimalist kind of teen. Your parents can leave Post-it notes with updates in a place where you will see them: bathroom mirror, refrigerator door, front door. Maybe something like: "Dad has chemo today. I'll be with him, so carryout dinner tonight."

"Sometimes teens find it easier to communicate with that minimal amount of information," says social worker Barbara Golby. It's not too much. It's just enough. You can leave Post-it replies and comments if you wish. Or not.

• •

Maya and Daniela's Story: Just Ask Us!

Picture this: Dad (that's me, Marc) is dragging in heavy bags of groceries on a cold, dark, rainy Saturday afternoon. Mom is upstairs in a deep chemo-instigated sleep. Maya and Daniela are watching TV.

Dad (exploding after he's made three trips in without any offers of help): "Can't you *help me with the groceries?!?*"

Maya and Daniela: "We'd be happy to if you'd ask us."

Dad: "D'oh!"

• •

//

Moral of the Story:

Both parents and teens may think that the members of your family can read their mind. If only it were so! When you were little, Mom and Dad might have said, "Use your words." That's still good advice for both generations.

//

Chapter 4

How Things Will Change During Cancer

The topic of this chapter: change.

❧ Changes in you: scared, mad, embarrassed, self-pitying, touchy, overburdened.

❧ Changes in your parents: all of the above, plus...the effects of treatment and *tons* of stress.

Well, if those changes don't spell out a recipe for good times, we don't know what would! But, in all seriousness, this chapter is here to give you a heads-up on changes to come and how to handle them gracefully.

• •

Rob's Story: You Can't Hide Burnt Oatmeal

Rob's mom was in bed, feeling lousy from chemo-therapy for her breast cancer. He asked if there was any food in the house for dinner. She said, "Yeah." But when Rob went downstairs, he couldn't find anything dinner-worthy. So he decided to make oatmeal.

Only Rob had never made oatmeal before. He didn't bother to read the directions on the box. He just put some oatmeal in a bowl, with no water, and put the bowl in the microwave.

"It caught fire," Rob says. "I was like, 'Oh no!'" He

took the bowl out of the microwave and put out the fire. "My clever way of hiding the bowl," he says, was to put it under a lawn chair in the yard.

Rob thought he was pretty smart, covering up his disaster. Guess again. "My grandmother found the bowl," he reveals.

• •

Rob's tale of oatmeal woe reveals a lot about what living with cancer is like, and about changes you and your family will face:

- Mom or Dad might not always be able to do the things they usually do.
- You will take on new challenges.
- You might get into trouble unless you *read the directions!*
- You might try to hide your failures—and also your feelings—from the adults in your family. Sometimes you can get away with it. Sometimes you can't.

4.1 Teenage Change Is Normal!

Change is scary. People of all ages are afraid of change. Yet change is part of your daily life. In fact, right now, change often seems to be the only constant: new teachers, new friends, new interests, new feelings, new realizations about what you want to do with your life.

During this teenage stage, your job is to separate yourself from your family and create your own grown-up identity. That means you

Words of Wisdom:

"Realize that your world is about to change dramatically, and accept it and embrace it and be supportive in ways that maybe you haven't been before. Realize that you may have to take on some responsibilities that you didn't have before. That this too shall pass."

—Pat Lee of Alabama, a single mother of two teens and a survivor of breast cancer won't hang out with your folks as much as you did when you were younger. It also means your parents will get on your nerves because they try to set rules and limits and curfews that appear to get in the way of the New You.

Marc and Maya say: We totally identify with this situation. We are father and daughter, and we both know the deal: from a teenager's perspective, parents can be incredibly annoying! From a parent's perspective, teenagers can be pretty annoying themselves. The psychologist Anthony Wolf summed it up in the title of his guide to raising teenagers: *Get Out of My Life, But First Could You Drive Me and Cheryl to the Mall?*

Keep in Mind: You may have already had some tough exchanges in the last few years. You and your parents may have had some shouting matches and quarreled and spoken harsh words that you later regretted. Doors may have been slammed. Punishments may have been handed out. It's all part of growing up, of being a normal teenager. Mom and Dad may not like this phase. You may not either. But there's nothing surprising about it—it's a tale as old as the first teenage rebel.

4.2 Cancer Sneaking Up on You

Now, suddenly, cancer arrives at your doorstep: a big, fat, unexpected, unwanted interruption. And nothing seems to be the same. That's what cancer does: it shakes things up. It introduces new worries and responsibilities. It is an agent of change.

There will be lots of changes. They will vary from family to family.

One major change, says psychiatrist Karen Weihs, is that the threat of cancer activates "the attachment drive." Humans are born with a drive that makes them want to be near something secure—maybe a place, maybe a person. When you're a little kid, you go out exploring in an unfamiliar environment, but if something scares you, you run right back to Mom and Dad.

"When cancer occurs in a family, everybody's attachment drive is activated," says Weihs. "They're more likely to seek connections with a parent, a sibling, a friend." For a teen, that means conflict because there are now two warring forces inside you: attachment drive vs. teenage stage of breaking away from your family.

So yes, there will be tensions.

There will be household changes as well. Maybe Dad isn't up to making dinner or driving car pool. Maybe Mom can't get to your ballet recital or soccer match. Maybe the parent with cancer will have less energy and look different—hair falling out from chemotherapy drugs, pale skin, tired eyes.

Or maybe you think your parents don't care about you sometimes or seem distracted.

"I felt like they weren't giving quite as much attention, but I knew in the back of my mind that their attention was being diverted into things much more important."

—Jake, thirteen, whose mom was diagnosed
with breast cancer when he was eleven

"The whole family has to live with the reality that life is uncertain. There are ongoing doctor's appointments; there are the side effects of treatment. The illness can impact the life of the family: everything from not being able to take a family vacation to changes in mealtimes and even in what you eat."

—Social worker Barbara Golby

Survival Tip: "Don't let [cancer] run your life. Let it be a part of your life."

—Emily, who was fourteen when her mom
was diagnosed with breast cancer

4.3 Changes to Expect

So your emotions will change. And all these emotions are totally normal. It's okay to be bummed out, mad, or disengaged. The key is to get support when you need it. (For more about that, see Chapter 11.)

Head Count: We asked fifty-three teens (and former teens) which of the following emotions they experienced while their parent was going through treatment:

- 61% felt depressed at times

- 52% felt angry at times

- 50% felt optimistic at times

- 48% were in denial at times

Normalize! Don't Feel Guilty about How You Feel

Therapists use the term "normalize" a lot. They want to "normalize" emotions. And you sure have a lot of emotions after a parent's cancer diagnosis that might not seem normal to you: mad at your mom or dad for getting cancer, mad that it wasn't the other parent, ready to put your siblings up for adoption.

So what does "normalize" mean exactly?

"The idea is not to feel as guilty, not to think, 'What kind of person am I for having those emotions?'" says psychiatrist Paula Rauch. "But instead to realize that people usually have some angry, negative, or critical feelings at times of stress. We are not in control of what we feel. That's just how it is. It is normal."

If you feel closer to one parent than the other and your super-close parent is the one with cancer, you may indeed wish the other parent was the unlucky one. "That's just natural," says Rauch. And it's very different from just randomly wishing that a parent was dead.

You might be angry at your parent with cancer at times, too. Also normal.

"It's a fantasy that people who love each other don't get mad at each other," Rauch explains. "In fact, you get mad at people you love because you expect a lot from them." So if you're mad at your parents even during cancer...maybe that just means you love them.

Although you do have to be careful about the words you speak in anger. Rauch notes the old but still very accurate saying: "Words spoken and eggs broken are not the easiest things to repair."

• •

You may find yourself responding to the new situation in any number of ways. Some teens do a disappearing act. They simply don't want to be home and face the fact that their mom or dad has cancer. They want to be out doing their own thing, hanging with friends, going to movies, participating in school activities, whatever they usually do after school and on weekends.

Marc says: Sometimes Maya and Daniela seemed oblivious to Marsha's cancer. In one way, that made me feel good—I didn't want them to worry all the time. But sometimes I wish they had shown a little more concern. I remember one freezing night in February when Marsha was in bed feeling lousy and I was running out to get her some ginger candies to see if they'd help. Maya was watching TV, and she looked up and said, "How's Mom doing?" And I was thinking, "Gee, maybe you could go upstairs and ask her!" I guess I should have shared my thoughts!

Maya says: I would definitely try to lie low when cancer was "in the house." When my mom got home from a treatment or was sick on the couch or when I could tell my dad was stressed, I would retreat to my room or try to get out of the house so I didn't have to deal with what was going on.

Being one of these Disappearing Teens doesn't mean that you're a bad kid or that you don't love your parents. It just means that this is the way you are coping.

Or you may be the Parental Helper. Willingly or reluctantly, you take on more chores at home and spend more time with your parent fighting cancer. "I tried to be super extra nice," says Jake. "I tried to always do what she wanted, like, right away."

Words of Wisdom:

"I often tell my clients that when the diagnosis comes, everyone kicks into gear, puts on their helmet, and is ready to go into battle."

—Oncology counselor Shara Sosa

As you may have guessed, change manifests itself in lots of ways.

"The family has to adjust to a 'new normal' of living with chronic illness," says social worker Barbara Golby. "It's not just the patient who's got to learn to live with that."

Or...What If Nothing Changes?

You know how there's an eerie quiet after a storm. The same thing might happen after the cancer storm strikes. Maybe your parents shared the cancer news and then everything went on as normal and you're like, "Um...do we need to talk about this stuff? Should I be crying?"

Chances are you don't want to be the one to "break the silence" and bring it up. Your parents may try to shield developments and emotions to protect you. Probably, they understand that being a teenager is hard and stressful, and they don't want to add to your heaping pile of things to do, places to be, and people to see.

Whatever the reason, you may want to know more about what's going on with cancer and your family. Maybe you like openness better than pretending that everything's fine despite the elephant in the room, aka cancer.

"My parents always pretended as if they were fine and everything was normal. It really bothered me because no one expressed any real fears or concerns out loud, and even if I did, my mother or father would brush them aside and would say everything was okay. In essence, I believe it brought secret conflict, even though our family came together annually to raise funds for the American Cancer Society through the Relay for Life event."

—Angella, nineteen, whose mother was diagnosed with breast cancer six years ago and is today a survivor

If you're wondering what's up, ask your parents if everything's okay or just for an update. (For more on communication, see Chapter 3.)

Most of you will experience changes, so here is a guide to some of the ones you may go through, brought to you by the kids who've been through them, along with advice from experts on how you can cope with the new reality.

4.3.1 Fear Factor

Cancer scares people of all ages. A Harris poll asked 1,007 people what disease they feared the most. The winner was cancer, named by 41 percent of the folks. And odds are that if your parents are scared of cancer, they've passed on that fear to you, too.

One thing that may make you less scared is accurate information. (See Chapter 3 for how to stay in the loop within your family.) Time helps as well. If your parent is moving through treatment and things look good, your fears may diminish.

4.3.2 Overburdened

Warning: more chores may be in your future. Everything from unloading the dishwasher to picking up younger siblings at school if you have a driver's license. You may feel resentful. Sometimes there may be no alternative, particularly in a single-parent household. "That can cause a lot of anger and frustration," cautions social worker Sara Goldberger.

Or you may just say "bring it on" so you can feel that you're helping. But

Words of Wisdom:
"What is ideal is for the child to take on some additional responsibilities but not to have to sacrifice the normal expectations for someone their age— they still get to go to the prom, do school sports, socialize with friends."
—Psychologist Barry J. Jacobs

if you do too much, you run the risk of being "parentified"— turned into a parental substitute. That's the topic of Chapter 5.

"It was an especially hard time during Mom's chemo, just seeing her like that. I would come home from school, and she would be on the chair in the living room, barely able to move, just feeling like crap all the time. So me and my sister definitely did everything around the house that we could."

—Travis B. of Manitoba

4.3.3 Walking on Eggshells

Toss cancer into any household and people will be on edge. "At the beginning I was really, really short-tempered," says Jake, thirteen, whose mom was diagnosed with ovarian cancer. "I think that was because I was scared."

Steven observed some mood changes after his dad was diagnosed with lymphoma: "Me and my family had the worst fights. About stupid stuff, too."

Unfortunately, the United Nations will not be able to send a peacekeeping mission to your home. So it's up to you and your parents to work things out.

Survival Tip: If you do something that you know really pushes your parents' buttons (like tracking mud into the house, leaving dirty dishes in front of the TV, or laughing in the face of curfew), consider cooling it to help tame the tension.

Give your parent a break in the same way that Mom or Dad might have given you a break in the past when you were stressed. "If your parent had chemo and radiation, they'll come home dead tired 'cause it just takes it out of them," says Travis W. of Utah, whose dad was diagnosed with a rare form of cancer. "A couple of times my father would get really mad over just the smallest thing that he would normally just pass by. So we had to be really careful!"

4.3.4 Self-Pity

Feeling sorry for yourself is normal. But wallowing in self-pity isn't going to help. "At the beginning you can feel bad for yourself," says Jake of Massachusetts, whose mother is a cancer survivor. "But try not to feel too bad for yourself. Instead, feel bad for the person who's actually dealing with cancer."

That's what Alison S. realized when her mother fought breast cancer and dad battled bladder cancer: "It's got to be way harder for them."

Besides, lots of kids have been in your position and have survived and even thrived. Vern Yip, the TV home designer, lost his mom to cancer and now gives an annual scholarship to a kid affected by cancer: "I am blown away by the strength of the human spirit," Yip says. "These kids' stories are never stories of self-pity. They talk about what they've learned, how they've channeled [the cancer experience] into something positive in their lives."

But that doesn't mean you can't have a short pity party, dedicated to the proposition that cancer sucks.

4.3.5 Feeling Helpless

You may also feel as if your hands are tied, powerless in the face of cancer.

"In some ways it's harder for family members who don't have the cancer," explains psychiatrist James Gordon, "because they feel kind of helpless. You do your best to help the other person do what's good for her, but you're not in control. That's another lesson you have to learn: ultimately even if you think something's a good idea, you can't make your mom or dad do it. You give them whatever advice you have, but they're gonna do what they're gonna do."

You're not going to be able to cure your parent's cancer, but that doesn't make you helpless. You can help by being there for your parents, helping out around the house, and being supportive of your siblings.

Coming up with a plan to deal with your anger and depression will also make you feel a little less helpless. See Chapter 6 to see what's worked for other teens.

4.3.6 JUST. PLAIN. MAD.

You may wonder: *why did this happen to me?*

Being angry that cancer happened to your family might turn into you feeling angry at your parents, your siblings, cancer itself, or the whole world. It's easy to start searching for culprits to take your anger out on. This might lead to family fighting, which only adds to the stress you're already feeling.

Words of Wisdom:
"If you don't talk about your anger, it can boil and boil...and then boil over. You'll snap at a teacher, wreck a friendship, do something dumb."

—Melissa Ford, school social worker

If you're angry, confide in a good friend. Try a support group. Write about it. Play video games. Do not punch a hole in the wall! (See Chapter 6 for more on how to cope.)

> "When my mom was diagnosed, I was in my room a lot. I hit a pillow. It felt good, but I was imagining that that pillow was cancer and I was going to squash it."
>
> —Jake, thirteen, of Massachusetts

4.3.7 Mad That You Can't Be Mad at Your Parents

You know that you can always get mad at your parents, and they'll still love you. But can you get mad a parent who has cancer?

. . . .

Mother-Daughter Story: Why It's OK to Get Mad at Mom
One teenage girl yelled at her newly diagnosed mom: "I can't even get mad at you now because you have cancer. So it's like if I get mad at you, I'll feel guilty and terrible."

"I think it can be really tough to rebel against somebody who's beaten down with cancer and chemotherapy," says psychologist Anne Coscarelli, who worked with that teenager and her family. "What's more," she says, "many adults will send a message to teenagers: don't get mad at your poor, cancer-stricken parent. How could you?"

But this girl did something really great. She shared her honest feelings with her mom. And the mom shared her honest feelings with the daughter.

Her mom said: "You can still get mad at me. Even though I'm going through a hard time, I'm still able to manage that you get mad at me. I'm sturdy enough. It might be hard for me, but I'm still your mom."

"The mother was able to recognize that it was a good thing that the daughter could say, 'I feel like I can't even get mad at you,'" Dr. Coscarelli says. That means the girl felt secure enough in her relationship with her mom to say what she was really feeling. And that's better than bottling everything up until it explodes. "It's more worrisome," says Dr. Coscarelli, "if a child feels that way and never talks about it."

. . . .

Marc says: That doesn't mean you should yell at your parents all the time. Give us a break once in a while. But yes, we're tough and we can take it!

Maya says: I remember that whenever I would get mad at my mom or dad or a fight would break out in our family, I would be overcome with this horrible feeling of guilt. If I could give any advice based on that experience it would be: a) Try to reduce conflict by letting things go or talking it out before you resort to yelling, and b) Don't let the guilt over your anger get to you too much. Getting mad at your parents is normal. Cancer doesn't mean that you're going to turn into a teen angel and never lose your temper.

4.3.8 Mad That It Wasn't the Other Parent

You know how it goes in your family. Maybe you feel close to both your parents. Maybe Mom really is your soul mate, and Dad not so much. Or vice versa.

What if the parent you feel closest to is the one who is diagnosed with cancer?

Sometimes in a support group, says child life specialist Kathleen McCue, "teens say to me in tears, 'I'm so ashamed. I feel so bad. I wish it was my other parent who had cancer.'"

Then they begin to cry, or they change the subject really quickly.

So what does it mean if you have these feelings? It doesn't mean you're an awful person. Sometimes one parent has said things that hurt you. You may be able to talk about that with the parent now and find some resolution. You may be able to forgive and forget. Or you may just come to accept that you have a different relationship with each parent, and that can color your reaction to the parent with cancer. It's perfectly normal. (See the sidebar on normalization on page 47.)

4.3.9 Jealous

As crazy as it sounds, you may be jealous that the person with cancer is getting lots of attention…and you're not.

That doesn't mean you're a bad person or you're not supporting your parent. It just means that you're a teenager. It's the stage you're in. You may have an important event coming up—a prom, a school trip, summer camp. And everybody's supposed to be paying attention to you. Only now they're paying attention to your mom or dad.

Meghan was definitely jealous when her dad was diagnosed with cancer: "It sounds so wrong. But I was jealous. My dad was the center of attention. I'm the only child. I should be the center of attention. When my dad got cancer, it was all about Dad, taking care of Dad. He got special candy because he lost so much weight from chemo. I was being forced to eat salads. I'm not saying I didn't take some of the candy—I was sneaking it. It was the jealous thing. I wasn't getting the special treatment. And because I like candy!"

Looking back, she says, "You might be jealous but don't feel bad about it. You're going to feel all this stuff. You will be okay." And then she adds, "I got enough candy."

4.3.10 Embarrassed by the Way Your Parent Looks

A parent came to talk to social worker Barbara Golby a few years ago with a sad situation to share. "I don't know what to do," the mom said. "My daughter is embarrassed that my husband has cancer. She doesn't want him to come to any school functions."

The mom felt like she was caught in the middle. She wanted to try to respect the wishes of her thirteen-year-old daughter, but she told Golby, "Frankly, I'm furious that she's excluding her dad."

"Younger teens, especially, have a hard time with parents coming to school with wigs and scarves and bald and sick and skinny," says Kathleen McCue. She thinks older teens cope better. But she does hear kids say they're embarrassed: "I don't bring friends over. My mom doesn't wear a wig at home. She looks weird." Maybe other kids at school are whispering about it: "Did you see Justin's mom? She is so bald!"

You may not be comfortable with the changed appearance of your cancer-stricken parent. But don't beat yourself up about it. "I think kids have every right to anticipate what their friends will think of the change in their parent," says McCue. "It's part of the dilemma: I want to fit in. I don't want to be singled out. I don't want to be the one who's different."

Ask yourself: "Is there a way that Mom or Dad can be a part of my life outside the house?" Maybe the answer is, "Yes, if you wear a baseball cap." Even if that isn't enough for you, you can tell your mom or dad: "You know I still love you even without hair." Also check out Section 4.4.1 for how other kids dealt with their mom's hair loss.

4.3.11 Closer to Your Parents

Most of the changes on this list are kind of...negative. But there are positive changes, too. Tyler R., now fifteen, of Virginia, had always been close to his mom. After his dad was diagnosed with cancer four years ago, he and his mom grew even closer. Tyler remembers lot of car rides when they would just talk and talk and talk. (See Section 3.4 on the therapeutic value of car rides.)

"We would tell each other things we couldn't tell anyone else," Tyler says. "I remember her saying that we were the only ones who understood what we were going through. Everyone else understood but they didn't quite understand the way we did."

That close relationship with his mom helped Tyler get through his father's cancer treatments. And it was helpful for his mom, too. Sometimes he'd give his mom a hug or a kiss on the cheek, or hold her hand, and that little gesture meant the world to her. "We were really there for each other," she says. "We were each other's rock. I don't know what I would have done without Tyler."

4.3.12 More Grown Up

When you have a parent with cancer, you are facing situations that your friends probably haven't experienced: a serious illness in the family, a shifting of responsibilities and priorities. So you may feel that you're "a little more mature," as Abby of Maryland, fourteen, puts it. And the result may be that your...um, immature...friends get on your nerves.

> "I have very short patience for people who act like they're five when they're fifteen."
>
> —Rachel, fifteen, of New York, whose mother died of breast cancer

If they're getting on your nerves, try to think back to You, Before the Parental Cancer. You probably were just like that.

4.4 Changes in Your Parent

The cancer itself might not change your parent. In many cases, no symptoms from the disease are obvious at the time of diagnosis. But the treatments sure can bring on changes. Surgery takes a toll on anyone's strength. Mom or Dad may lose their hair—and some of their energy—to chemo. Radiation can cause fatigue as well. If your parent is battling brain cancer, there might be a change in personality as time goes on.

All those changes are now a part of your life.

"Your parents might start to act different, might not be able to do everything they used to be able to do, might start to look different. There's no reason to be worried because it's gonna happen whether you're okay with it or not. It's just going to happen. You'll make it easy on yourself if you look at it with a positive attitude, not sit there and think, 'Why did this happen to my parents? Why didn't it happen to somebody else?' Try to be positive, try to help out in whatever way you can."

—Tyler R., who was in middle school when
his dad was diagnosed with lymphoma

4.4.1 Hair Today...

If your parent is going through chemo, their hair is likely to go, since many chemo cocktails wipe out hair cells along with cancer cells. Dad will join the Vin Diesel/Samuel L. Jackson/Bruce Willis no-hair-for-men club. Mom will rock the bald head in the best tradition of actresses like Natalie Portman, Charlize Theron, and Sigourney "Alien" Weaver, who shaved off their locks for a movie part.

Mom or Dad may cry or feel very self-conscious about the bald head. For many cancer patients, the bald head is a signal to the world: I've got cancer and I'm going through chemo.

Or maybe your mom or dad will laugh at the absurdity of it all.

"My mom has an amazing sense of humor. She can laugh about anything. When she knew she was going to lose her hair, she shaved the sides like a Mohawk. She used my brother's colored hair gel. For Christmas, she wanted a reggae hat with fake dreads in the back. She would be like, 'Do you think people think I really have dreads?' I was like, 'Mom, no!'"

—Alison S. of Washington State

• •

Megan's Story: Giving Mom a Mohawk

Megan Boyer, thirteen, shaved the hair off her mother's head using an electric clipper first, then a razor and shaving cream. Stacy Hoover, forty-two and a single mom, knew the hair was going to be gone soon anyway. Here's how mother and daughter remember the moment.

Stacy: "I asked her if she wanted to, and she was like, 'Let's go now!'"

Megan: "[Doing it myself] made it fun. If she would have let it all fall out, that would have been a little scarier."

Stacy: "I was hoping she wasn't going to cut me. She was gentle, a little afraid. When she was just a little girl, I let her shave my legs in the shower. So I felt safe."

Megan: "I was nervous when she gave me the razor. She told me I could do whatever I wanted. I gave her a Mohawk at first."

Stacy: "I looked in the mirror and laughed. I was a funny-looking mom. [Having Megan shave my hair] helped me get through. And I didn't look all that bad without hair."

• •

"We'd just got to the hospital. We brought dinner. Dad went to sit up and turned his head, and half his eyebrows flew off."
—Tyler R., fifteen, of Virginia

So what could Tyler and his family do? "It was just one of those things. You laugh at a certain situation you normally wouldn't laugh at—because you don't want to cry."

And so Tyler and his parents laughed at the vanishing eyebrows. Hair loss, however, isn't the only physical change that you will see in a parent undergoing chemotherapy. A number of other physical side effects also can occur.

Maya says: I remember feeling kind of self-conscious about my mother's bald head—for example, when friends came over, even close friends. A bald head is just a very obvious, in-your-face symbol of cancer. At the time, I always felt bad for being self-conscious about it, and I would never have openly said something or admitted that I wasn't comfortable with her bald head.

Marc says: Actually, I think Mom had a really cute bald head!

4.4.2 Energy Crisis

Just the stress of diagnosis can make your parents tired—both the parent with cancer and the caregiver parent. Then come the treatments.

How tired will your parent with cancer be? "Chemotherapy-related fatigue is like ten times tired," says psychiatrist Paula Rauch. A nap or even a good night's sleep won't necessarily help.

What you have to remember is that energy is like "money in the bank," says Rauch. You can't spend energy you don't have, and you need to make an "energy plan" so you spend your energy wisely.

So maybe your mom or dad will tell you: "I don't have much energy, so I don't want to use my energy nagging you about doing chores or homework. I'd rather use that energy to watch our favorite TV show together or come to your dance recital or soccer match." That's not always possible. Your parent might tell you: "I'd love to have the energy to go to your games, but right now I just don't. I'm looking forward to going when I'm done with chemotherapy."

Or your parent might make a supreme effort.

"My mother had just had surgery for breast cancer," says

Emily, who was fourteen at the time. "I was one of the leads in *Fiddler on the Roof* at school, and I was just being a total jerk. I wanted my mom to come because *I wanted her to come.*"

Looking back, Emily knows she was being way too demanding. After all, her mom had cancer. But when Emily was singing one of her songs, she looked down into the audience: "There was my mother, in the third row, just looking like death." But nonetheless, there she was.

Seeing her mom in the audience changed Emily. Instead of being a typical teenage brat, she says, she became much more supportive of her mom.

P.S. Kids, your own energy may be a bit down because of the stress of Mom or Dad's cancer. Jake remembers how it was for him when his mom had cancer: "I went outside less. I was playing with my brothers less. I was just too tired emotionally to invest in anything else."

Keep in Mind: Under the best of circumstances, your parent only has so much energy. That reserve of energy will probably diminish during cancer treatment. Maybe that energy needs to go toward working. Some cancer patients go to work just about every day during chemo, either because of financial necessity or because the routine of a job offers a sense of normalcy and accomplishment at a time when everything seems out of control.

4.4.3 The Great Mood Swing

Mom or Dad may be a touch more moody with cancer. You can blame that on a number of things. For example, the fatigue brought on by chemo can make a patient likely to nap during the day, which interferes with nightly sleep. Also, the patient may not feel as strong or look as good as before treatment. And in the case of breast cancer, the patient may be mourning the loss of a body part to surgery.

And don't forget...just being the parent of a teenager can

make someone irritable. "It's hard enough when we have all our faculties," says oncologist Lidia Schapira.

You can offer support—maybe just sit and watch a movie with your tired, irritable parent.

Marc says: Be the nice guy. Let Mom or Dad pick the movie.

Or maybe the parent needs to be left alone for a while.

> "Everything made her irritable. When you're upset, every-thing gets on your nerves. You don't want people to bother you. I'm very talkative; I love to interact. It was hard for me to learn to shy away."
>
> —Jaclyn of Louisiana, describing her reaction
> to her mother's breast cancer treatment

If your parent has brain cancer, you may see other changes. "People can't walk as well, think as well, and there may be some personality or temperament changes," Dr. Schapira notes. Keep in mind that brain cancer is an uncommon cancer with only about 20,000 cases a year.

In some instances, high doses of medication can affect a parent's behavior as well.

If your parent is saying or doing things that don't seem typical, you can tell yourself what Reilly of Virginia would tell himself when that happened with his dad: "It's the cancer talking."

4.5 Siblings

If you're lucky, you and your sibling(s) have a great relation-ship and can lean on each other for support.

But it's quite possible that you and your siblings routinely squabble and tell on each other and even sabotage each other with cruel practical jokes.

Maybe you can mend fences. But sibling tensions are inevitable. And you can't force your brother or sister to behave as you think they should. Maybe they're always out of the house during the cancer months because they don't want to face your mom or dad's cancer head-on.

But some things can be addressed. For example: unfair division of household chores.

At the very least, you can enlist your parents to help with that matter. Together, the family can make a list. Post it on the refrigerator. Be specific: Suzi takes out the garbage before 6 a.m.; Chad will empty the dishwasher before going to bed.

If you're an older sibling, you may assume a protective role over your younger siblings and provide some support that previously your parents may have provided—from homework help to giving them a ride to a friend's house. If you're an older sibling who's providing a *lot* of support, you may be at least partly parentified. (See Chapter 5 for more on that.) Or maybe, your little siblings look up to you for support. "I tried to put on a bold face for everyone, including my little sister," remembers Luz of Virginia, whose mother was diagnosed with breast cancer when Luz was thirteen.

And vice versa: if you're a younger teen with a kind older sibling, you may be able to look to them for extra support or guidance.

Words of Wisdom:

"What I tell the dutiful kid is that when all is said and done, you will have your own sense of knowing you did the right thing."

—Social worker Lynnette Wilhardt

> "If they're older siblings like me, I'd tell them it's definitely okay to feel bad. But at the same time, you need to set an example of strength for younger siblings. They will look up to you for support."
>
> —John of New Jersey, who at fourteen was the oldest of three kids when his mom was diagnosed with breast cancer

And as we said a few paragraphs ago: remember that siblings are very different. You and your brothers or sisters might react and deal with your parent's cancer in totally different ways.

"It was so hard for Jennifer (the older daughter) to digest that she would retreat into her friends," says dad Don Fisher, whose wife battled cancer, "while her younger sister was so worried that she would be home every afternoon with her mother." These differences don't mean that one of you is right, the other wrong, or that one of you better than the other. You're just different people and are going to deal with the situation differently.

• •

Sibling Story: When You All Don't Get Along
Mom was diagnosed with Stage 4 breast cancer. Lyndsey, sixteen, became the family caregiver. And she was not happy with the way her younger brother, Lance, fourteen, was acting.

"He's an asshole," she ranted. "He doesn't do anything to help. He makes the worst mess and leaves home and does nothing. Mom was really sick in March. I asked Lance to take the garbage out, and he dumped it on the kitchen floor. He's very angry. I hope he understands she has cancer." What's more, Lance basically left the premises. He moved in with a buddy for a couple of months.

Here's what Lance says: "When I first found out, I was at my friend's house a lot. I didn't want to be home. I didn't want to see Mom go through that stuff. She would be crying, acting different, and little things made her mad." So yes, he definitely knew his mom has cancer.

How do siblings bridge this kind of gulf? "It helps

if the parent or someone in the family can help the siblings understand that we're all going to react differently," says social work professor Victoria Rizzo. Based on the way your sibling is acting, you may think he or she does not care. Rizzo notes: "That's not necessarily true."

Your sibling may care a lot—but just express it in a different way, perhaps with denial, perhaps by staying away because he or she can't bear to be home at this difficult time. As for Lance, he did move back home. Now he says: "I hate to see how other kids disrespect their parents and treat them like crap. I used to be mad at my mom. Now I spend time with her. It's brought us closer."

• •

• •

Hanging On to the Way Things Were

In this new reality of changes and unknowns, how can you *and* your family preserve a semi-normal family life?

You may be worried about losing the ability to be a regular, red-blooded teen. Will you be able to keep up your everyday life? Will other people notice something's up? You may start to grow up a little faster and that's okay. And you may find that you and your friends no longer have as much in common. "Sometimes kids who have a family member with cancer don't care to go hang around the mall, go to that party, pick out the latest fashion," says child life specialist Sandi Ring. "They're really worried about much bigger things. The kids struggle with still wanting to be just normal kids."

Don't stop hanging out with your friends, don't disengage from school, and don't quit all the activities you've become involved in. It's okay to continue on with your life. Try to make space for Your Normal Teen Life as well as your new role as the child of a parent with cancer.

To maintain normalcy at home, keep communicating (see Chapter 3) and don't let family traditions, habits, and rules fall to the side.

Chapter 5

PARENTIFICATION

Help! I've been parentified!

"Parentify" is a word you've probably never heard. If you go on dictionary.com and type it in, or try to find it in your mom or dad's beat-up *Merriam-Webster*, you'll get no results.

If you could find it in a dictionary, you'd see something like this:

par*en*ti*fy (verb): A term used by therapists to refer to a role reversal in which the child feels he or she is taking on responsibilities that normally fall to the parent.

As you have probably guessed—or know from personal experience—cancer can cause parentification. It doesn't happen to everyone, but when it happens, you may need help in handling this unexpected change in status.

5.1 How It Happens

A very dutiful teen may actually want to be parentified. Stepping up to the parental plate may seem like the best way to help out. Other times, parentification is thrust upon a kid—especially in single-parent families. There may be no other adult who can pick up the slack. But parentification isn't exclusively a single-parent family phenomenon. Even in a two-parent family, a teen might be parentified.

"Sometimes dads can't cope," explains psychiatrist Karen Weihs. "They just stay at work all the time, and the kids are at home and have to slog through on their own." Or Dad may turn to the daughter in the family for the kind of household help and emotional support he would seek from his wife under normal circumstances.

So the thirteen-year-old is fixing meals and doing dishes. The sixteen-year-old is picking up younger siblings from school and play dates, and the eighteen-year-old may have to help Mom to the bathroom if Mom is feeling weak from chemo.

Taking on all that responsibility may be the only way your family can get through the cancer crisis. But that doesn't mean it's easy. You are making sacrifices. "You are deprived in certain regards," psychologist Barry J. Jacobs says. "There's a certain lost innocence." As a teen, you may not have the time (or energy) to do the things your peers are doing.

Keep in Mind: "Cancer in general takes away childhoods," social worker Seth Berkowitz says. "It can rob children of innocence. Try not to let it rob them of the things teenagers like and need to do." That's not to say kids shouldn't take on any caregiving tasks. "In some ways, it's a good therapeutic coping skill," says Berkowitz. It's a good thing if kids have the urge to help out and figure out a way to act on that urge. "My concern," he says, "is always when they are *the* caregiver."

"Everyone else was going to the movies and mall, and it was like 'I've got to stay home and help take care of my sisters.'"

—Bailee, who was twelve when her mother was diagnosed with breast cancer

"I didn't want to leave everything up to my mom. Whatever she didn't do, I tried to help her with. Loading the wash, taking care of the dog, feeding the cat—basically whatever needed to be done I tried to do to the best of my abilities."

—Tyler Reeder

"Tyler turned into the man of the house. I would say he was very brave about it. He would help take care of the dogs and cats, help do laundry, step up and help cook. He'd do things around [the house] that he normally wouldn't do. I think in little ways he was Cindy's crutch."

—Chuck Reeder, Tyler's dad, who survived cancer

• •

Lyndsey's Story: Only 16, Acting Like She's 40

Lyndsey already had a pretty full plate before her mom, who is a single parent, was diagnosed with breast cancer. Lyndsey excels in her classes, plays on sports teams, takes ballet, and has an active social life. She is busy, busy, busy.

Now Mom is undergoing chemotherapy to fight her cancer, which has spread to other organs. Mom is also going to work every day. Lyndsey has two younger brothers, fourteen and nine. She gets up, "makes muffins, pours cereal, leaves a note for the brothers." Later in the day, she says, she'll check in with her mom to see who will pick up her brothers from school.

Lyndsey sums up: "I have to cook, clean, and make sure my mom eats and my brothers are fed."

The demands on Lyndsey seem as if they'll never end. "I hate it when I'm doing something like mopping the floor and my mom is like, 'Can you get me a drink of water?' And she always has to have a straw."

If Lindsay forgets the straw, her mom may say, "I'm not going to live that long anyway."

Lyndsey and other parentified teens sometimes feel that they have two different ages: their chronological age and what they call their "cancer age."

"I'm sixteen," says Lyndsey, "and I have to act like I'm forty."

• •

5.2 Catching a Break

The key is to find a balance so you, as a teen, aren't parentified 100 percent of the time.

Maybe relatives or good-hearted neighbors and friends can pitch in. If the adults in the family can figure out a plan, then they can say to the teen, "Go have fun!"

That's how Bailee's mom did it. She relied on the kindness of friends to give twelve-year-old Bailee days off from caring for her two younger sisters. "All my mum's friends were so good about it, too," Bailee recalls. "On the weekend they would be, 'Okay, we'll take the girls.'"

Bailee, who's now seventeen, remembers how it felt to get weekends off: "Just to go be twelve again, that was really quite a blessing. The friends would step in for an entire weekend. It doesn't seem like much, but when you're dealing with [cancer] every day, to be allowed to be a kid and be yourself for a weekend is absolutely awesome."

Some caregivers—adults as well as teens—may find the idea of a break to be stressful in its own right. "People get so identified with this heroic role that they don't want other people to step in," says psychologist Barry J. Jacobs. "They're resistant to giving up certain chores that they're doing." In this kind of situation, he says, the parent should "forcefully limit how much a particular child is doing."

A Dutiful Son's Story: To Party or Not to Party

Years ago, Dad had cancer. Now his son was twelve, and the cancer came back. The boy told his mom, "Now I have to be the man of the house."

"He put a lot of those responsibilities on himself," social worker Marisa Minor says. She talked with his parents about giving him permission to be a kid. When he'd say, "I don't want to go out with friends," or when he wanted to stay home, she talked with his parents about the importance of encouraging him to go out anyway. "There was a time when he was fighting with them. He didn't want to go to a party all his friends were going to." But his parents prevailed. He went to the party.

"Afterward, he said he was glad he went," Minor says. And he was glad his parents had recognized that he needed a break.

"I help cook. I help clean the house. And sometimes, I feel like I'm the man of the house because my stepdad can't be there all the time, even though he tries to be there as often as possible."
—Jaclyn, the Louisiana teen whose mom had breast cancer

"January this year was really hard on my family. Everything gets put on me. I try to stay strong for my brothers. I'm so caught up being mom to my brothers *and* my mom."
—Lyndsey, sixteen, of Virginia

Dear Parentified Teen:

If your parent wants you to take a break, don't fight them. Besides, any caregiver will tell you that it's all too easy to burn out. Relaxing will give you some much-needed "me time." The question for all caregivers is: how do you keep on being a caregiver? How do you "replenish yourself for the caregiving mission?" Jacobs says.

And if "me time" is hard to find in your household, request permission to gripe. To vent. To complain about how unfair it all is. Because, really, it is just not fair. Now, it's true that complaining won't change anything. But you may feel better if you let your resentments out rather than bottling them up.

Dear Mom and/or Dad:

"If the kid is angry, acknowledge that it's okay to be angry," says social work professor Victoria Rizzo. "And make sure the kid has enough money and time to at least go to the movies with friends."

• •

Stacy and Megan's Story: A Grateful Mom

"There were times when I was at my wit's end, wasn't sure if I was gonna be able to manage," says Stacy Hoover, a single mom who was treated for breast cancer while working full-time and being a parent to two daughters: thirteen-year-old Megan and a one-and-a-half-year-old.

Megan became more than a big sister. There were diapers to change and the inevitable toddler's outbursts to cope with. "Sometimes I wanted to go over to a friend's house, but I didn't want to leave my mom with the baby," Megan recalls. "There were times when she was getting chemo that she was irritable. It was hard for me not to yell back.

"I wanted to yell back a lot of times. Sometimes I did, but I felt bad."

Stacy Hoover had her rough patches as well. "There were times I just couldn't help it, times I'd snap and didn't mean to. I wanted to assure her it was the medicine and it wasn't me. I wanted her to know that I couldn't help it. I just always thanked Megan, made sure she was aware I was grateful for what she was doing for the household and how she helped out with the baby."

• •

• •

The Toll That Caregiving Can Take

In some cases, caregiving can be incredibly intense — and can leave a lasting impact on the young caregiver. Psychologist Barry J. Jacobs, author of *The Emotional Survival Guide for Caregivers*, is now counseling a twenty-one-year-old who spent the past two years of his life caring for his grandfather, who was battling severe lung cancer. The grandfather had raised his grandchild, so Grandpa was really a father to the boy. And the grandchild became the parent to his beloved grandfather.

"He made a commitment to be with his grandfather through his illness, to the very end," says Jacobs. The grandson saw his grandfather delirious. He saw him losing control of his bladder and bowels. Now the young man is haunted by the memories of his grandfather's illness. He can't get the thoughts and images of what he saw out of his head. "He literally has post-traumatic stress disorder. He was really, really traumatized," says Jacobs.

"It would have been better if someone had said to the grandson, 'No, you can't be there,'" says Jacobs. Only there was no other family member in the picture.

This isn't a case of full-blown PTSD, Jacobs notes. But kids who have helped care for a dying parent, or even a grandparent, "may have really intrusive visual images and thoughts of the person at the end of their life."

These images can affect you for years to come, distract you from other pursuits, or make it hard just to do the things you need to do, like studying or socializing.

This kind of experience isn't limited to teens who've cared for a dying parent. "Seeing parents suffer from the side effects of chemotherapy—vomiting, hair falling out—can have psychological consequences," says Jacobs.

This is a case where the parents of the teenager might not be able to help. But by seeing a therapist or attending a support group, the teenager may be able to come to terms with what he or she has seen. "The key is not to try and push the scene away," says Jacobs. That kind of denial can make it harder to put the scene in perspective.

Putting your feelings into words is helpful as you try to find some meaning in what you've been through. "You can learn to acknowledge the intrusive thought but not have the reaction of high anxiety," says Jacobs. "You can say, 'Yes, I witnessed this and survived it.' It gives you some appreciation for life, a knowledge that other people your age don't have." And that may allow you to understand things in the future that other people can't understand.

• •

5.3 Silence Isn't Golden

If you're feeling compelled to take on responsibilities, you may also feel obligated to hide sadness or anger from your parents.

"Many of the kids report not wanting to talk," says mental health counselor Mae Greenberg, "and not wanting to share their feelings because they don't want to upset the parents." Or maybe you don't want to cry in front of your parents.

Mental health experts say: Don't try to stay strong and keep everything inside. You're allowed to cry. And it's healthy to express your feelings.

You may also feel you can't talk to your parents anymore about little problems you're having. How can you bring up a fight with a friend or a hard test in the face of a parent's cancer? The answer is: you can and you should! Your parents are still your parents, and you can go to them with your normal issues. They probably want you to.

"One of [the] main things we want kids to know," says oncologist Mary Hardy, "is it's okay to talk with their parents about a prom dress or something mean someone said in school. You might think it's not important enough to bother Mom or Dad with, but they would love to deal with a problem like that. That's what parents do."

5.4 THE BIG PICTURE

What happens to a parentified kid years later? "There are long-term effects," says psychologist Barry J. Jacobs. These kids are at risk of becoming adults who are "codependent"—who are always looking for someone to take care of.

That might be a problem in personal relationships but not in other ways. "I will tell you, lots of people in the health-care professions had a childhood experience of taking care of a parent or grandparent," Jacobs says. "These are the kids who grow up to be therapists, doctors, nurses." The trauma they witnessed and the caregiving they experienced has had a lasting—and positive—effect.

Chapter 6

DEALING WITH STRESS

Teens find many different ways to handle the pressures of a parent's cancer. Some of these coping mechanisms may make you feel better but could cause problems. You twirl your hair...until it falls out. You get drunk, then get pulled over while driving and are slapped with a DUI. You scrawl graffiti on a school wall and get caught. Other coping mechanisms can help without posing any risks: music, sports, writing in a journal, going to a support group, just talking things out with a close buddy.

This chapter will deal with positive ways to cope.

Survival Tip: "Live, laugh, and love are the three most important things to do while your parent has cancer. You need to live long, laugh hard, and love a lot."
—Travis W., sixteen, of Utah. His dad was diagnosed with cancer ten years ago and has defied predictions of an early demise.

6.1 HOW TO BEAT THE CANCER BLUES

If you figure out what de-stresses you and makes you happy, you'll be better able to cope with bad stuff in the years ahead.

These activities will keep you in a good frame of mind and offer relief in times of stress. You'll pour yourself into them when the going gets really tough.

Your body releases a hormone called cortisol when stress hits. Cortisol has all kinds of negative effects on your body. "People need to de-stress so their hormones revert to lower level," says psychiatrist Paula Rauch. "Otherwise there are all kinds of tension-related challenges—tight muscles, stomachaches, headaches."

Words of Wisdom:

Reading a book is one of the most powerful ways to escape from your troubles. "If you're really into the story and your mind doesn't wander," Paula Rauch says, "then you leave the stress behind. People can also get the same kind of escape from movies or music that tells a story."

"One of the important life skills," she affirms, "is figuring out what works, what you do when you're sad that helps."

> "I love reading, and that was one thing that helped me stay calm."
>
> —Jake, thirteen, of Massachusetts

> "Do not focus on the cancer. Try to keep your life as normal as possible. Keep playing sports or instruments, going out, or doing whatever it is you do. Do not let the cancer dictate your life."
>
> —Callie, who was seventeen when her mom was diagnosed with pancreatic cancer. Her mother is a ten-year cancer survivor.

You don't necessarily want just one go-to behavior. Psychologist Anne Coscarelli adds, "For kids as well as adults, people who cope better have more than one strategy."

There may be times when nothing helps. Lyndsey, who's sixteen and whose mom has metastatic breast cancer, went for a run with her coach and just started bawling one day. Did crying make her feel better? "No," Lyndsey says emphatically. "When it's bad, you don't feel better."

But you shouldn't stop trying to find things that help you cope.

6.2 EXPLORING THE OPTIONS

So where do you start? The list of possible coping mechanisms goes on and on and on: listening to music, writing music, writing in a journal, going on a run or a bike ride, shooting hoops, meditating, watching TV, talking to someone, learning magic tricks, baking cookies, playing video games.

Your parents and other adults may offer suggestions. Maybe their ideas are good. Maybe not. "There's no shortage of misguided adults," psychiatrist Paula Rauch says. "Find a coping mechanism that works for you, not one that works for Mom and Dad. Figure out what you enjoy, what makes you feel better, and then consistently incorporate these strategies into your everyday life."

Still, it can't hurt to have some ideas to choose from. We asked experts for their suggestions. Of course we asked teens as well.

6.2.1 SPENDING TIME WITH FAMILY AND FRIENDS

Just hanging out with family and friends, doing what you did before cancer, is a great way to maintain a sense of normalcy.

> "What helped me a lot was just doing the stuff that I've always done with my family."
> —Tyler T., fourteen, of Utah, whose mother was diagnosed with breast cancer when he was in the fifth grade

You know who makes you happy. And who doesn't. Make an effort to spend time with the people who boost your spirits.

"For most people it's really good to have somebody to talk to," says psychiatrist James Gordon, founder and director of the Center for Mind-Body Medicine. "Otherwise you feel so alone with these feelings, like you're the only person in the universe who's ever been through this. And you're not. It's good to feel that connection with others who have enough life experience to have been through dark and difficult times. But they have to be people you feel comfortable with."

6.2.2 Writing and Drawing

Express yourself. You can do it in words, in a journal, or by drawing pictures.

"All of these are ways to get out what's inside," says James Gordon, who writes about strategies that can help you deal with a difficult situation in his book *Your Guide to the Seven-Stage Journey Out of Depression*.

Artful coping: what strategy did you use?

❦ "I'm a rhymer and a rapper. At the end of the week, I'll sum up everything in a poem or rap. I'll put it on Facebook. In one rap, every line starts with 'why.' Like, 'Why is it when I pray I don't get an answer?/Why did my dad have to die of cancer?'"
—Steven, whose father was diagnosed with cancer when Steven was fourteen and died a year later

❦ "I kept a diary through the whole thing. I still have it in my room. Just every day, when I came home after the hospital, I shut myself in my room and turned on Pearl Jam. I wrote about: 'Why did this happen to me?' I kept track of everything the doctor said. Since I didn't want to talk to anyone, that was my form of dealing with it. Writing definitely helps. I could tune out everything and just write and write and write."

—Morgan, whose father was diagnosed with cancer when she was sixteen and died within a year

"I didn't like to talk much. I would just draw a lot. I drew what I was feeling. That really helped me cope."

—Luz of Virginia. Her mother was diagnosed with cancer when Luz was thirteen and is today a survivor.

6.2.3 GET PHYSICAL

Think of your body when you are feeling down. You're kind of slumped over. Your head is hanging low. When you're scared, your body shuts down, your emotions shut down, and your mind stops working.

Psychiatrist James Gordon's prescription: "Put on hard-driving rhythmic music and shake your body. Stand up with your knees bent and shake from your feet on up to your shoulders. Shake for five minutes. Dance to music that really moves you. If there are words, they should be words that inspire you. As you change your body's stance by moving it, your emotions change along with it. That can be very helpful if you're going through difficult times."

"I've loved to dance ever since I was an itty-bitty girl. Our garage has really smooth floors. I'd [put on] my music and dance my heart out. It was a good reliever of all the questions, stress, emotions I had built up inside of me. I let it out. Nobody could see me in my little zone."

—Jaclyn of Louisiana. Her mom was diagnosed with Stage 3 breast cancer when Jaclyn was thirteen. Five years later, Mom is in good health.

If dance doesn't turn you on, you can find lots of other ways to move.

"Being active is a great distraction," advises psychiatrist Paula Rauch. "It often engages you with other people, and it often makes people feel much better. There's good evidence that exercise helps people with their moods."

Many teens agree. Sports have done it for them, helping them release the negative energy building up inside.

> "When I'm outside, I get away from everything, you know. You actually see how big the world is. It just calms you down to see how amazing everything is. I've been on a mountain and looked and seen how big the area is and how cool it is. You see something that blows you away."
>
> —Lance of Virginia, whose mom has metastatic breast cancer

Testimony: what helped you cope with your parent's cancer?

✗ "Running is a really big stress reliever for me. I get past two and a half or three miles, and nothing else really matters. I run every morning before school. It wakes me up, keeps me going."

—Reilly, sixteen, of Virginia

✗ "A lot of surfing. I would go out on the water. It was peaceful and all kinds of animals are out there, like seals. It was really a good place to clear my head."

—Ryan Urich, whose father was diagnosed with cancer when Ryan was a teen

✗ "Football was—and still is—a [release] for any problem. I'm a quarterback. When I'm on the field or doing what I have to do related to football, I don't think about anything else. Football is my time of peace and serenity, and it always has been—especially when my dad was sick."

—Tyler R., fifteen, of Virginia

✗ "Soccer is my life. Playing soccer got me through lots of things."

—Molly, fourteen, of Virginia, whose
mom is a breast cancer survivor

• •

True Story: A Soccer Star's Saving Grace
James Riley found out that his mother had been diagnosed with breast cancer when he was just starting his freshman year at Wake Forest University. "That was a shocking phone call," he recalls, "and it was probably the last time I cried that hard, hearing those words—I have breast cancer—come out of her mouth."

Riley considered dropping out of school and coming home. His mother (a single parent) was back home in Colorado Springs while he was hours away on the East Coast at school. Being far from home made him feel helpless. But he ended up staying at college.

Talking to his coach, family, and family friends helped reassure him and make him feel better. But soccer was truly his saving grace. "Soccer was a place where I could get away," he says. "Leave all your baggage outside the soccer field and step into the lines. That time where you can have a break and be creative and enjoy the game and competing."

Now, he uses his role as a professional soccer player to help other kids going through the same experience, working with organizations like Susan G. Komen for the Cure and Gilda's Club Seattle.

His advice for teens? "Be life giving every day, not life taking. Do things you love. Enjoy life and enjoy those around you."

• •

6.2.4 Don't Forget to Breathe!

Another prescription from psychiatrist James Gordon: "I'll teach people slow, deep breathing. As you learn how to quiet yourself down, you balance out fear with the relaxation response. Sit quietly, breathe deeply in through the nose and out through the mouth. Let the belly be soft.

"First of all, that takes you out of that frantic state. Second of all, it helps to clear your mind so you can think more clearly. If you're less overwhelmed and more in control, you're more able to deal with whatever comes up.

"If you feel despairing or wind up crying, sit there and breathe, and that helps you move through those dark places and the anger. Breathing deeply and relaxing is a kind of anchor in your body. You're in the here and now as those emotions play over you.

"Just start by doing it for five minutes a couple times a day. Then if you're feeling upset, you can make a decision based on what feels right to you: get up and do the shaking and dancing [see the first suggestion in Section 6.2.3] or sit quietly and breathe. Both of them will get you to the same place."

6.2.5 Gaming Can Be Great

Luz didn't want to talk to friends about her mom's breast cancer. She didn't want to see a counselor or write about her feelings in a journal. What she did want was to play video games. And not just any video games. For Luz, who was thirteen when her mother was diagnosed with breast cancer, the games had to be violent.

"That," says the soft-spoken Virginia teen, "helped me cope." Her game of choice was the Ninja warrior game Naruto. "There's a lot of button frenzy," she says. "It felt good winning. I felt the vibration in my hand when the enemy got hurt."

She pauses. "Sounds cheesy, I know."

Actually, it's not cheesy at all. While many adults (and even Congress) thinks violent video games promote aggressive behavior, a new study shows that the games can help relieve stress.

Public health researcher Cheryl Olson, cofounder of the Center for Mental Health and Media at Harvard Medical School, was the principal investigator for the Grand Theft childhood study, named for the ultra-violent video game that has gotten a lot of bad press.

The study looked at 1,254 students in seventh and eighth grade who were video-game players. The idea was to look for potential negative results of playing but also to understand why teens play violent games.

The teens reported that they played to get their anger out, to forget their problems. They played if their parents were having a fight, and they played if they had a bad day at school, if the teacher yelled at them for forgetting their homework.

"One said he used a cheat code to get a tank and ran over everybody, including someone who looked a little bit like his teacher," says Olson.

After the teens played, they said they felt better, calmer, less inclined to lash out physically or verbally. They felt in control.

The study did not specifically look at teens coping with a parent's cancer, but you can connect the dots. Playing a video game can help.

Now that's not an endorsement to play 24/7. If you're playing video games in all your free time and shunning friends, if you're avoiding things you used to like doing and staying shut up in your room, that's a sign that you could be depressed.

But if video-game playing is not taking over your life, then it can be a kind of therapy. "It helps you block out the world and vent your stress and experience the opportunity to feel in control and blow up something that you know is not really hurting anybody," says Olson. And of course, nonviolent video games also can help to take your mind off the stresses in your life.

A video game can also connect you to Mom or Dad. Invite them to play with you. Tell them you'll show them how. They'll probably mess up, but maybe sitting side by side, you and Mom or you and Dad will laugh at how bad your parent is at video games. And maybe you'll find it easier to talk about other stuff—how your day was, and what you're thinking about the cancer.

6.2.6 Tune In

Sometimes you don't have to do something active to cope. You can just listen. Put on your earbuds and listen to a favorite song on repeat, or get into a singer or band. As long as you aren't wearing the earbuds 24/7, it's fine to escape from your woes by getting into a song.

6.2.7 LOL!

A little laughter can help you feel better. But humor doesn't just drop out of the sky. Seek it out. Watch a funny movie, go to a comedy show, read a funny book, or just engage in goofy activities like a family game of charades.

> "There was so much tension and nervousness in the family. Me and my sisters would sit down and watch some cheesy movie and laugh really hard."
>
> —Luz of Virginia

• •

Jackie's Story: Cracking Up, in a Good Way
Eighth grade was not a fun year for Jackie. Her dad was dying of cancer, and her mom had also been diagnosed with cancer. After her mom told her the news, Jackie went to school and told her friends everything. "I was

like, okay, my mom has breast cancer." One friend looked at her and said, "Cancer hates your family."

Now that kind of comment could bring a teen to tears. Only here's what happened: "We all cracked up," says Jackie. "We really cracked up. We should have been really sad, but we all really cracked up. My mom says, if we can laugh at it, then we're not crying."

• •

Of course, another great way to cope is reaching out to other people, which we'll talk about in the chapters coming up.

Chapter 7

RISKY BUSINESS

A parent's cancer can affect you in different ways.

It can lead you to become a better you—stepping up to help care for Mom or Dad, taking on more chores at home, gaining an appreciation of how precious family really is.

Or it can send you spiraling into self-destructive behavior: Drinking. Drugs. Hooking up. Vandalism. Arson. Theft.

No statistics are available to show how many teens get into trouble after a parent's cancer diagnosis. Plus, teens get into trouble in families without cancer. So it's hard to know: if you're acting out, is it because of Mom's or Dad's cancer, or would you have gotten into trouble anyway?

All we can say is: sometimes teens turn to a risky behavior that might feel as if it helps them cope with their feelings in the short term.

"Drinking until you pass out may numb the pain, at least for the moment," says someone who did just that when she was a teen and her mom had cancer. "But I would *never* advocate this."

Here's what some teens (and adults looking back at their teen years) have to say about the things they did when Mom or Dad had cancer—and how they managed to turn their life around.

7.1 Former Bad Boys: Gary and Jose Turn It Around

This is a tale of two boys. We'll call them Gary and Jose. For a while they were in the same support group for teens coping with a parent's cancer. And one night they each shared stories about the things they did wrong, and what helped them find new ways to cope.

Gary, fifteen, describes himself as "funny and helpful and kind." Until recently, he lived with his grandmother. His mom and dad are out of the picture. So Grandma is like a mother to him. She was diagnosed with cancer but at first she didn't tell him. When her hair started to fall out from her chemo treatments, she couldn't hide it any more.

Now, after many months, she's still fighting, still going through chemo and not strong enough to take care of her grandson. Gary has moved into the basement of a neighbor's house.

After his grandmother was diagnosed, Gary got into trouble. For starters, he missed school. And there's a lot more: "I was doing stupid things—doing drugs, getting into a lot of fights, doing vandalism, running from the cops."

He was caught and put on probation.

"I had anger," Gary says, "and I didn't know how to release it."

Oh, and because life is supremely unfair, Gary is also a childhood cancer survivor. He's okay, but he walks with a bit of a limp because of the bone cancer he fought—and beat—some years ago.

A teacher at Gary's school recommended that he drop in on a support group. And Gary found out that talking about his anger helps him.

Gary was also inspired to turn his life around by an ex-girlfriend who had a baby. Seeing the change in her life made him realize that he wants to "grow up," he wants to be able to buy his own stuff. He quit smoking weed about five months ago, and he's working hard to do well in school and "get it together." He's also found some legal ways to deal with his pain. Like bowling. "It makes me feel better that I've got something to do instead of sitting around. It gets my mind off it."

Jose goes to the same support group that Gary goes to. Jose's mom has cancer. Grandma was the one who told him. He wishes his mom had told him herself but says he's okay with the way it played out.

Cancer bummed Jose out. He was smoking weed, ignoring schoolwork. "I gave up on everything—school, grades."

Then he decided to turn himself around. He started reading the Bible, and he stopped smoking. And he found ways to let out his feelings: dancing, boxing, sometimes just walking around.

"I'll just walk back and forth. My mom is like, 'What are you doing?' But walking back and forth actually does help."

Both Gary and Jose sound a bit wistful when they talk about their use of marijuana. They miss it a little because they both say that smoking a joint sometimes helped them forget about cancer for a little while. But they seem glad that they've stopped and found other ways to cope.

7.2 FORMER BAD GIRLS: TRUE CONFESSIONS

Boys aren't the only ones who act out. As a matter of fact, a study on adolescent reactions to a parent's cancer found that girls were more likely to have behavior problems than boys.

A teen we'll call Janey was in seventh grade when she found out her mom had breast cancer. That was five years ago. "I was pushed into the role of being a second mom." She just wanted to be a kid. "I drank and did drugs," she says. "That's not being a kid." She just wanted to forget. Did it help her forget? Janey's head drops and tears well up in her eyes: "Not really."

And then there's Elissa.

Elissa is a poster child for risky behavior. She was in middle school when her mom was diagnosed with cancer. Her parents were going through "an ugly divorce."

"I remember being very angry," says Elissa, who is now thirty. "No one was watching out for my needs. I was twelve and very demanding. I needed a lot of attention. There was a school dance I wanted to go to. I remember asking my mom. She said, 'Ask your dad.' He said, 'We'll have to see how your mom's feeling.'"

Elissa was very frustrated. No one wanted to help her make plans to get to the dance. And that was just one cause of her frustration.

As Elissa remembers it, her mom stopped being a mom. The live-in nanny took care of Elissa and her older twin sisters. "At the time, it felt like every man for himself in my house," she says. "We were all jockeying for the very little attention and resources our parents were giving us." She jokes that she stopped going to the dentist when she was twelve. Elissa says, "Our parents stopped parenting us." That didn't mesh well with the mindset of a teenager: "When you're a teenager, you want what you want when you want it."

The lack of supervision, says Elissa, meant that "she did some things I shouldn't have gotten into. I was looking for attention in all the wrong places." Those "things" included drugs, alcohol, and a relationship with a man twelve years older than she was. Elissa says that although she was twelve, she looked like she was eighteen.

She had a fake ID. She'd go out and no one would ask where she was going or when she was coming back. She forged her mother's signature on notes to get out of school thirty-six times in just one semester. When the school caught on and called her mother, her mother didn't feel up to going to school to discuss the problem.

Looking back, Elissa wishes she had had some positive outlets for her anger. Drinking, drugs, and sex, she says, "numbed the pain" but ultimately didn't help.

At fourteen, she had purple hair and piercings, and she smoked two packs of cigarettes a day. At sixteen, she had a baby. Her boyfriend was mad that she had pregnancy complications and had to go to the hospital on his birthday. He went out to celebrate.

Things got worse. After Elissa had the baby, her boyfriend grew angry at her one night. He pushed her down the stairs and threw a glass coffee table at her. It shattered everywhere. Elissa remembers thinking, "What the hell am I going to do now?"

What she did was make a decision: "I am going to turn this around." She took and passed the test for a general equivalency diploma, enrolled at a junior college, transferred to Georgetown University, graduated at age nineteen, and went on to graduate school at Johns Hopkins University. At age twenty-three, she herself was diagnosed with breast cancer, and then again at age twenty-five. A two-time cancer survivor, she now runs a program for breast cancer survivors to address their medical and emotional needs after treatment.

Looking back at her wild youth, does she know what might have helped?

"I needed assurances," she says. Assurances that her mom would be okay and that there were parents to care for her even in the middle of this medical crisis. "I felt like no one really talked to me."

She wanted to know: what was her mom going to go through? Would her mom be a survivor? What does it mean to be a survivor? And what would their family life be like in the short run and the long run?

She didn't want her mom to sugarcoat—just to tell it like it was. Without information, Elissa remembers, she'd veer between thinking her mom was going to die and thinking, "Well, she'll be just fine."

For teens who find themselves in the bad way that she did, she says, "Try to bring your parents in. Find ways to express your needs. And I'm a big fan of finding someone to talk to outside the house, a third party who's objective—maybe a social worker or psychologist."

She and her sisters are all doing well today. "We have all gotten through it," she says. "But it was definitely a tumultuous few years." And it didn't have to be that way.

• •

How to Fix the Hole in the Wall—and Feel Better in the Process

A lot of boys punch holes in walls. And by "a lot" we mean almost every boy we interviewed. Punching holes in walls might not be as risky as experimenting with drugs, but there is potential for harm to a) your hand (look out for studs!) and b) the wall. So why do boys do it? And is there an alternative?

Experts recommend taking a swing at a punching bag.

But let's say you didn't listen to the experts.

You punched a hole in your wall.

You can hang a poster over it. You can push a bookcase up against it. Or you can fix it.

It's not that hard, and it won't cost that much—maybe $30 in supplies and a couple of hours of your time. Pat Sandor, a product expert at Home Depot, gave us the step-by-step for fixing a four-by-four-inch hole—"a standard fist hole," he notes.

- Buy a wallboard repair patch: that's a thin perforated piece of rustproof aluminum, four inches square, with self-adhesive on the back. "Take the adhesive off and literally stick it straight over the hole," Sandor says. And spread a drop cloth so clean-up will be minimal.

- Buy some sheetrock all-purpose joint compound, aka "mud." Sandor recommends about a quart of heavy or lightweight mud. With about fifteen strokes of a stir stick, "spin the mud to smooth it out," Sandor says.

- Spread the mud with a sheetrock taping knife. "Get a knife as wide as the repair so it covers the entire hole," says Sandor. Maybe an eight-incher. Dip the knife into the sheetrock mud, start at the edge of the repair patch, and spread a thin layer across. Then add another layer, coming from the opposite angle.

- Strive for an even coat. Then take a break. Drying time: about two hours.

- Once the mud is dry, smooth it out. A sanding sponge will absorb excess mud, which you can wring into a bucket.

- Paint it! You can get a match for the paint by going to a paint store with a piece of the paint that came off when you punched it. Apply paint with a white foam roller.

- Not only will the wall look okay, but you might feel better, too, when you're done. "I don't mean to play therapist," says Sandor, who is a scoutmaster in his spare time, "but it's therapeutic for that young man to do the repair himself." Added bonus: you'll have gained a skill that will be of value for a lifetime—maybe even when you grow up and have angry, hole-punching teenagers in the house.

· ·

Chapter 8

The Power (and the Limits) of Optimism and Faith

How do you find the strength to cope with a parent's cancer? Friends and family might give you the support you need. Maybe a couple of hours on the soccer field will enable you to recharge your batteries. Or maybe you look to other sources: your head and your heart, your religious faith.

You'll hear a lot of talk about attitude and hope, about optimism and spirituality. What you don't always hear is that cancer can test everything you believe about positive thinking and religion.

8.1 Think Positive

People will tell you many things about cancer that aren't true.

One of them: optimism can cure cancer.

It can't.

"Unfortunately there is no study that supports the notion that cultivating optimism will give you a better outcome," says oncologist Lidia Schapira.

Sure, everyone knows a person who was given a slim chance of surviving and who had the most optimistic attitude ever and who somehow managed to beat the odds and is alive and well today.

Surgeon Sherwin Nuland, a professor at Yale University School of Medicine, wrote about such a patient in his award-winning book: *How We Live.* Her name was Sharon, and her diagnosis was devastating: a sizeable tumor in her breast and cancer in her lymph nodes as well. Dr. Nuland believed she had a one-in-four chance of surviving for five years. Yet she was a twelve-year survivor when he published his book. He wrote that "keep[ing] yourself positive" is definitely a good thing for the patient, in terms of quality of life and maybe even in terms of longevity. But at the end of the chapter he observes, "For every Sharon, I have known a dead optimist."

Yet people will tell you: chin up! Think positive thoughts!

Words of Wisdom:

"Everyone has different ways of coping with adversity," says Cynthia Lofaso, a professor of psychology at Central Virginia Community College. "There is a tendency for people who are well-intentioned to try to put on a positive spin or to downplay the negative or to encourage people to have some sort of an optimistic outlook. That's not necessarily appropriate for everybody. It's not a coping style that works well for everybody, teens included. It is okay to have bad days and it's okay to be sad and it's okay to struggle."

The tyranny of positive thinking also makes people feel that they're not supposed to "consider the possibility of a dire outcome," says psychologist Barry J. Jacobs. "That's just not realistic."

8.1.1 THE DOWNSIDE OF POSITIVE THINKING

That leads us to a phrase that psychiatrists and psychologists and social workers use when they talk about cancer: "The tyranny of positive thinking."

Huh? How can thinking positively be like a tyrant, an unfair ruler, and something that is bad for the cancer patient, the caregiver, and the family members?

The reason is that people have a range of emotions when they face cancer. If you feel as if you have to smile through it all and hide negative emotions, the negative emotions don't go away. They stay bottled up inside, making you scared and nervous and generally upset. Talking about them, on the other hand, can be helpful.

When a cancer patient—or a family member like you—is made to feel that having doubts or negative thoughts is a bad thing, when you have to be upbeat Tigger all the time and can't let your inner Eeyore out, "this is not useful advice," says psychiatrist Paula Rauch. "It's not how people function." People don't have just one feeling and that's it. "They have lots of feelings. You feel different ways at different times. It's not authentic or a good coping strategy to just have one emotion."

In other words, you don't want to force yourself to be happy. "Give yourself permission," says Rauch, "to feel what you feel."

• •

Janis's Story: Honest Mom Sets the Tone

Janis Moore, a single mom in Maryland, wanted to set an optimistic tone for her kids, including thirteen-year-old Paul, while she was being treated for breast cancer. She went to work every day during chemotherapy.

"If I felt good enough to go to work, in his mind that day was a good day," she says.

But she tried to be honest as well as optimistic.

"When I told them I had cancer, I vowed I would do everything within my power to beat it, to return to normal. I lived by that," Moore says. But she also recognized that there are some things in life you have control over and some things you don't—like cancer.

Her kids understood her perspective. She didn't hide her feelings from them, says son Paul. "And I didn't try to hide anything from her." Paul also found ways to cope with his feelings of sadness and depression. He began going to a teen support group. He came to see that staying in his room and bottling up feelings was, for him, a "bad way" to cope. A good way? "Go to your mom or guidance counselor and just talk. Talking about it helps you get over things."

• •

False optimism can backfire. If the kids get only optimistic reports, even if the parent with cancer isn't doing well, that can be devastating as well.

"My dad fought really hard, and he was really optimistic," says Mansoor of New Jersey, whose dad battled colon cancer for five years. "He was never not optimistic." Mansoor's parents would only give him good news updates. Which meant he could "pretend" everything was fine. No worries!

If he suspected that bad news had been received, "I'd have to read it through how my parents were acting." That was confusing. "It was," Mansoor says, "kind of a guessing game."

In households where only optimism is expressed, the kids may also feel pressure to be upbeat all the time.

> "I remember always having to be upbeat around her. If I was sad, that wouldn't help her. That's too much of a burden to put on yourself."
>
> —A Virginia teen, whose mother was diagnosed
> with stomach cancer and died a few months later

8.1.2 WHERE POSITIVE THINKING COUNTS

That's not to say optimism is a bad thing.

> "I believe a lot in the power of positive thinking. My mom was always like, 'It's going to be fine' and she was just, 'Keep up your positive attitude.' And even if things start to go for the worst, take advantage of the time you have."
>
> —Kelly of Maryland, whose mom was diagnosed
> with breast cancer. Mom is now in good health.

Optimism can make you (and your parents) feel better. "When people are miserable, they are miserable," psychiatrist Paula Rauch says. "There's no advantage to being miserable." Even at a low point, if you and your parents can find reasons to feel grateful for little things, that might help make all of you feel a little bit better.

Worst Thing I Heard:

"A friend told me that my mother had cancer because God was punishing my family for being atheists. Someone at my high school told me that I made God give my mother cancer by being bisexual."
—An eighteen-year-old whose mom has been coping with metastatic breast cancer for seven years

"Some people said she shouldn't have surgery. It will probably go away on its own with positive thinking. Surgery is the easy way out."
—A woman who was a teen when her mom was diagnosed. The mother did have surgery for breast cancer and is today a survivor.

And you may feel better if your parent is optimistic. But psychiatrist Paula Rauch has only one caution: "Optimism is great as long as it does not shut out space for worries and doubt."

Marc says: The doctors were optimistic about Marsha's prognosis, so we tried to set a positive tone in our home when she was going through treatment. That doesn't mean we had to be optimistic 24/7. But maybe 23/6?

8.2 Faith and Spirituality

"I'll admit there was a point when I was mad at God," says Luz of Virginia. Her mom was already dealing with diabetes…and then was diagnosed with breast cancer.

"I was very angry," Luz confesses.

That was a tough moment for Luz, who was raised with strong Catholic beliefs.

When cancer comes into a family, many people who have deep faith find themselves at a loss. How could this happen? Your mom or dad may ask that question. And you may ask it, too.

It's a tough place to be: a test of faith, a crisis of spirituality, a time when you wonder whether prayers can help, whether God is listening.

People may say to you, "God doesn't give you what you can't handle." And you may be thinking, "Yeah, but cancer still sucks."

"I don't hear as many kids saying [they] use their faith," says child life specialist Kathleen McCue. "I hear adults say it. Kids are struggling with the dilemma of why God lets bad things happen. It's a real teenage thing to say, 'I don't believe in God anymore.'"

8.2.1 "It's Okay to Be Angry"

That's what Luz's mother told her: "Everyone can get mad at God." It's okay.

Chaplains who work with cancer patients and their families will tell you the same thing.

"If somebody's really focused on, 'I'm angry at God, good. That's fine,'" says Rev. George Handzo, who has served as pediatric chaplain at Memorial Sloan-Kettering Cancer Center. "Be angry at God. I'm not going to try to talk you out of it. God can take it."

Besides, he says, if you believe that God knows everything

you feel, "Why fake it?" Being angry at people that disappoint you "is a normal human emotion."

"Don't let anybody say to you, 'Oh, you shouldn't be angry at God, you're not being a good Christian, Jew, Muslim....'

"Be angry at God. You have every right to be angry. Sure, we wish that God would have kept this from happening. But God didn't."

And the question is: then what? Can you get over your anger? Can you still draw comfort from religious faith, from praying to God on your own or in church, from going to religious services or a religious community, or both?

8.2.2 AFTER ANGER, THEN WHAT?

Luz is no longer angry. Time helped. So did the support of her friends and her mother, who had taught her that it's not good to hold a grudge, that hate is "the worst thing you can have in your life."

Today, Luz's mother is doing okay. After surgery and chemotherapy, she is in remission. "My bond with God grew stronger," Luz says. "I have a stronger faith and a strong belief in miracles." But it doesn't always work out that way.

8.2.3 WHAT CAN YOU PRAY FOR?

People of faith wonder: does prayer help? Chaplains ask that, too. So do doctors and scientists, some of whom have tried to see if they can prove that prayer does—or doesn't—make a difference for people struggling with a health problem

Michael Eselun, a chaplain at UCLA's Jonsson Comprehensive Cancer Center, says that if a cancer patient or family member asks him about prayer, he asks them: what does prayer mean to you?

If the answer is that your idea of prayer is asking God for

help, for a miracle, then Eselun might ask: so then why isn't the whole world healthy—and thin and good-looking?

He remembers a twenty-eight-year-old man with leukemia, a tough guy who was a bare-fisted boxer and also very reflective. This young man said, "I could pray for God to heal me. But why me and why not everybody on the floor with cancer, why not the kids with cancer downstairs?"

Michael Eselun adds to that: why would God need your prayer to know that you love your mom and want her to hang around and be there for you on your graduation day? "To say, 'Please give me that' is deeply human—and a deeply naïve view of life. The notion that if I ask just in the right way, I'll get it."

Instead of praying "for" something, he proposes thinking of prayer as a way of trying to listen to God rather than making a request. And maybe the act of praying will give you the strength you need to cope with your parent's cancer.

On the other hand, Chaplain Yusuf Hasan, who counsels patients at Sloan-Kettering, says: "Pray and don't be afraid to ask God for help."

"I always try to encourage [people] to pray for what they want, for what is realistic," he says. So you might pray for your mom to get her hair back, to be able to go out with the family again.

Survival Tip: *Meditation.* Maybe you've heard about meditation. Maybe you like the idea. Maybe you think it's a little strange. But if you're curious, try it. Create a place in your head where you can go to calm down, suggests oncologist Mary Hardy. You could be thinking religious thoughts or just trying to quiet your mind. Maybe a little meditation will help you deal with the stress of Mom or Dad's cancer. (See section 6.2 for more ideas on how to cope.)

But no one can tell you what to pray for. "The answer lies within you," Chaplain Hasan says.

And what if you pray and you feel your prayers aren't answered because the cancer doesn't go away or it comes back? Hasan says he would only be able to say to that person: "Sometimes if we pray, we can see the answer. Sometimes we can't. That doesn't mean the prayer doesn't get answered. My thing is for them to realize there's another existence that comes into play." So you might not see the answer to your prayer in this lifetime, he says.

And he emphasizes: "We don't know the answers to all these things."

Chaplain Handzo makes the same point: you can pray for whatever you want to pray for. But he cautions: "That doesn't mean you're going to get it, and it doesn't mean there's anything wrong with you if you don't get it. But you can ask. There's nothing wrong with that. I think prayer can help if your goal in prayer is not answers but comfort."

8.2.4 THE POWER OF PRAYER

If you or your close ones pray for your parent, will it make a difference? That is a question you may ask yourself as your parent goes through cancer treatment. It's a question doctors have wondered about as well.

> "My faith played a large role. I attribute my [mother's] survival to nothing but God and having hope and faith."
>
> —Jaclyn of Louisiana. Her mom was
> successfully treated for breast cancer.

When you pray for someone else, it's called "intercessionary prayer" or "distant prayer." The word "distant" doesn't mean that you have to be many miles away from the person you're praying for. It's just the way academics refer to this type of prayer—by someone other than the patient.

If you look on the Internet, you may come across different studies on distant prayer. One study from 1988 got a lot of attention at the time and for years after. Randolph Byrd, a cardiologist at the University of California at San Francisco Medical Center, studied 393 heart attack patients. He divided them into two groups. He asked "participating Christians" to pray for patients in one group but not in the other group. And his study reported that the patients in the "prayed for" group fared better.

But there are problems with such studies.

Richard Sloan, a professor of behavioral medicine at Columbia University, explains: "Distant prayer is impossible to quantify. You can never know who's praying for whom."

Besides, another study had seemingly opposite results. Herbert Benson, director emeritus of the Benson-Henry Institute for Mind Body Medicine, set up a study of 1,802 patients who had undergone coronary bypass surgery. He had three groups of patients who had gone through bypass surgery for a heart problem.

He asked people to pray for one of the groups. He did not ask anyone to pray for the second group. And then he set up a third group, and he asked people to pray for the individuals in that third group. And while he did not inform Group 1 and Group 2 whether they were being prayed for (or not), he told the members of Group 3 that people were going to pray for them.

So who would do best? You might think that the people in Group 3 would have the best recovery because a) people were praying for them and b) they knew it.

Here's what the study found: Group 3 was the group that did the worst, according to results published in 2006 in the *American Heart Journal*.

The doctors who worked with the study aren't sure why. Maybe the people in Group 3 were nervous because they knew someone was praying for them. Maybe they thought: Gee, am I in such bad shape that they need to have people pray for me?

Or maybe getting back to Richard Sloan's point: It's just impossible to know.

Chapter 9

The Benefit of Friends

If you're lucky, you will have supportive, understanding friends to help you get through this time. You also might encounter some less-than-awesome friend situations. This chapter will outline some of the possible social scenarios you may encounter and some ideas on how to deal with them.

Remember how scared you were when you first heard the "c" word? Your friends are probably scared of it, too. Or they might just be scared they'll say the wrong thing to you.

If you have one or more best friends or a close circle of friends, you'll probably let them know what's up. Hiding your parent's cancer from them would be a challenge. You'd have to banish your friends from your home and tell lots of white lies. Not to mention that your friendship support network would consist of you, yourself, and you.

> "My friends were so awesome. My better friends would notice when I was a little tentative and would ask if something was wrong. Even though I would always say 'No,' it made me feel better to know they might be thinking of me."
> —Jake, thirteen, of Massachusetts

> "I was at boarding school, and my roommate was the only friend I told. He probably didn't understand [what I was going through], but he felt sympathetic. I remember telling

him he couldn't tell anybody else. I don't want to feel pitied. I didn't want people to change their relationship with me."

—Hakeem, sixteen, of Virginia, whose
father died of pancreatic cancer

Head Count: How supportive were your friends?

- 45% said their friends were "somewhat helpful"

- 30% said "they were always there for me"

- 25% said "they just didn't understand"

9.1 What You Do (and Don't) Want from Your Friends

You know the expression: "Can't live with them, can't live without them"? Sometimes you may feel that way about your friends.

Can't live without 'em: You love your friends and you need them and you just want them to be there for you.

Can't live with 'em: But…they always seem to say the wrong thing and act the wrong way when it comes to your parent's cancer. Maybe they're so wrapped up in their own teen troubles that all they do is complain about boyfriend or girlfriend problems, mean teachers, and zits—which are pretty trivial compared to coping with a parent's cancer. That could make you feel alienated from them or angry at their…teenager-ness.

Even though your friends may have the best of intentions, they probably don't know *how* to be there for you in the exact way that you want. That's a dilemma that many of you will face.

"There's one friend I've always been open with," says Travis B. of Manitoba. His mother had been diagnosed with cancer and eventually died of the disease. Travis's buddy had his own tragedy: his mother, who had struggled with alcoholism, had died a couple years before. "If I didn't have him, I probably wouldn't have been able to get through it," says Travis. "Once or twice I cried in front of him, and he didn't think any less of me."

9.1.1 PITY EYES

So what do you want from your friends?

Actually, let's start with what you don't want: "Pity eyes."

That phrase was used by several teens we interviewed. As in: "I hate it when someone looks at me with 'pity eyes.'"

You probably know what they mean from firsthand experience. It's that look you get when you tell a friend about your parent's cancer or even if you haven't say anything but they still know. They furrow their brow, make a little frown, and widen their eyes so they look like Bambi when the hunters shot his mother. "You know, when they just don't know what to say and look at you all sad," says Kelly of Maryland, whose mom had breast cancer and is now in good health

The intentions are good, but pity might not be the intention you're looking for.

> "I hated it when people pitied me. I just thought that was weird. I hated it."
> —Allison B., thirteen, of Idaho, who lost her dad to prostate cancer

Fact! Pity comes from the French word for compassion. So "pity eyes" are just a person's way of showing they care and have compassion for what you're going through. They don't mean to come across as annoying or rude.

9.1.2 UNWANTED EXPRESSIONS OF SYMPATHY

Every teen can tell you what they don't want to hear from their friends.

A girl at a support group in Columbia, Maryland, delivered an oral dissertation on the subject.

"I hate it when people say, 'I'm sorry.'

"Why are you sorry? You're not God. You didn't cause it."

"I hate it when they say, 'I know how you feel.'

"No, you *do not know how I feel.*"

We could write a whole chapter listing all the things that friends said that ticked off the teen whose parent has cancer.

"My grandmother had cancer." *Not the same.*

"My dog had cancer." *REALLY not the same.*

"Oh yeah, my aunt had that same kind of cancer. And she died." *Really, really, really not helpful.*

> "People at school ask, 'Why is your mom so lazy? Why doesn't she do anything? Why is she so crabby, really tired? Why is she bald?' If you know my mom has cancer, leave it be. Why are you so in my business? Let it be, leave it alone."
>
> —Lyndsey, sixteen, of Virginia, whose mom was diagnosed with Stage 4 breast cancer

As we will note over (and over and over) in this book, people don't all have the same reaction to the same comment from a friend. "I'm really sorry," might sound genuinely comforting to you. Or it might sound comforting one day and then make you say, "Shut up" the next day.

"It doesn't help when people say, 'I know what it's like,'" says Jackie, fourteen, of Ohio. "They did not have the same experience." That's a bit of an understatement. Jackie's dad was diagnosed with cancer, fought it, but passed away. While her dad was battling cancer, Jackie's mom was diagnosed with breast cancer. Mom is now doing well.

So what does Jackie want to hear? "I find it comforting when people say something like, 'I don't know what it's like, but I'm here to support you.'"

9.1.3 WHAT IS THE "RIGHT THING"?

"Try and flip it around," is what social worker Sara Goldberger tells both adult cancer patients and their teenage children who are confronted with a friend who says the wrong thing or else just doesn't know what to say.

She'll ask a teenager: "What would you have said a while ago if your friend came up and said, 'Oh my God, my dad was just diagnosed with cancer'?"

A lot of people are stumped and can't come up with anything, she reports. "And they realize saying the right thing is not as easy as it sounds."

> "Find supportive friends and dump the ones who aren't. If they don't support you in the hard times, they aren't really your friends."
>
> —A twenty-nine-year-old who was fourteen when her mother was diagnosed with breast cancer

Do you have to tell your friends what you want to hear? That's a big burden. You don't want to have to go around school being the Great Cancer Educator. If a casual acquaintance says something you don't find especially helpful, maybe you can just shut it out. "But for key people you feel particularly close to," says psychologist Anne Coscarelli, "you could share information about the kind of support you need."

That teenage girl from the Columbia, Maryland, support group knew what she wanted friends to say: "Do you feel like talking about it?" Because sometimes she really did want to talk about it.

Words of Wisdom:
"If you say to your friends: 'Don't ever mention this,' they're not going to. And if you wish your friend would ask you how you're doing, you're going to have to tell them. Your friends can't read your mind!"

—Child life specialist Kathleen McCue

And if she didn't, then she wanted them to say, "What do you want to do—go to the mall, go for a bike ride, just hang out?"

You can also tell anyone right off the bat that you just *don't* feel like talking about it. Sara Goldberger suggests trying out this line: "I don't want you to ask me all the time. I'll let you know when I need to talk."

> "Here's one possible response to a question you'll get a lot: 'How's your mom (or dad) doing?' I always said: 'She's doing very well—thank you for asking.'"
>
> —Emily, who was fourteen when her mom was diagnosed

> "Friends always try and help out, but unless they've been in the situation themselves, it's hard for them to identify with how you're feeling."
>
> —Samantha, twenty, whose mother was diagnosed with breast cancer three years ago and has been told by doctors she now has about two years to live

For friends who don't know what to say, Sara Goldberger says they probably can't go wrong with the generic "Boy, that sucks." It acknowledges what you're going through without the friends trying to pretend that they can relate or they've been there.

Survival Tips: Here are some things to figure out for yourself and then tell your friends:

- **Talking about it.** Do you want them to know and never bring it up again? Do you want them to talk to you about it only when you bring it up? Do you want them to check in with you to see how you're doing? How often? What do you want them to say?

- **What not to say.** If certain phrases or questions really bother you, tell your friends this so they know not to say them. For example, if you never want to hear, "I'm so sorry," or "I feel so bad for you," tell your friends that these phrases are taboo!

- **Telling others.** Do you want to swear a couple of close friends to secrecy: "Don't tell anyone else what I said"? Or do you want them to tell other friends for you so you don't have to? And keep in mind that swearing someone to secrecy doesn't guarantee that the secret will be kept.

- **Being there for you.** How can your friend be there for you? Do you want to schedule weekly dinner dates or jogs or sleepovers?

- **Support.** For really good friends, could they or their families provide any support to help you and your family? Do you need rides to school? Do you want to be able to go to their house when you need to get away? Do you need help with your homework? And if you don't know what you want, that's fine, too. Just let your friends know that you're trying your best and will keep them posted if you need a hand.

Once you figure out what might work for you, give your friends some direction so they can be there for you in the "right" way. And you might offer different directions to different friends. You might want much more conversation and support from your best friend in the world than from a casual buddy on your soccer team.

The best time to share this information is when you first tell them so they get the right idea from the beginning, before they start to get on your last nerve. You can tell them in person or send them an email or even go very old-school and write them a letter.

If you want to tell a friend what you need, either in person or via text or email, keep it simple and straightforward.

You might try something like this: "So you know my mom (or dad) has cancer. I'm still dealing with a lot of it, and I don't want to talk about it all the time. But I'd really appreciate you being there when I do."

> "Friends did the best they could. I realized it was unfair to expect them to really be able to understand what I was feeling. But no question, they were there for me. I could call them. Hanging out with them was nice. It was nice to get away."
>
> —Brett B. of California, whose adoptive mother was diagnosed with lung cancer when he was seventeen

> "Stick with your core group of friends, people you know will always be there for you. If they're into sports, get more into sports."
>
> —Reilly, sixteen, of Virginia, whose dad died of cancer two years ago

Every friend is going to be different. Some might be natural supporters and others might not have the slightest clue about what to do. Jenny of Massachusetts says, "One friend was really supportive—she was always over at my house, knew how my mom was doing, was very cool with whole thing. Another friend was like, 'Oh, are you going to be different now?' That's not a helpful reaction."

9.1.4 SILENT SUPPORT

Sometimes all you will want from your friends is a quiet understanding of what you're going through. For them to just keep being your friends and act like everything's normal.

That's what Morgan of Washington wanted. Her friends hadn't dealt with what she was dealing with: her dad being diagnosed with cancer and not such good news about his prognosis. "My friends were there for silent support," she says. They were by her side at school, and they'd say, "If you want to talk, we're here. If not, that's fine, too."

9.2 GIRLS ARE FROM MERCURY, BOYS ARE FROM NEPTUNE

Mental health experts who work with teens do think that gender can influence what you want from your friends.

Girls tend to want their friends to express sympathy and talk to them about what's going on.

Boys tend to want their friends to treat them as if nothing's changed.

Then again, we did meet a lot of girls who wanted their friends to act as if everything was the same. And we met boys who wanted a friend to confide in.

So maybe it all comes down to your personality and your mood at any particular moment.

What annoys girls: "Many times," says psychiatrist Paula Rauch, "girls will talk about how their friends either don't ever get it or move on to other topics very quickly. And how hard it can be to have their friends talking with great distress about much lesser challenges."

9.3 ACCEPTING HELP

Try not to be too proud to accept the help and support of others! If your friends offer assistance that you truly do need, humble yourself and say "yes." It'll make them feel good, and it might do you some good, too.

"Don't shut people out," says Pat Lee, a breast cancer survivor in Alabama who's a single mom with two kids, Rob and Alex. "When people want to help, let them. When your friends and family rally around and want to do everything for you, it can be difficult to accept. Let people help because they want to. They love you and it's a good thing. So let people help you. Embrace it. Accept it."

9.4 Have Fun with Your Friends If You Can

Friends can be a tremendous help for teens when they need to spend some time not thinking about their parent's cancer.

> "My friends helped me realize I do deserve to have fun. I can't just feel guilty over things I have no control over. And that I should get through school to the best of my ability and have fun and be aware [my friends will] always be there for me."
>
> —Kaitlin, fifteen, of Ohio, whose mother died two years after being diagnosed with cancer

At least every now and then, let yourself forget about the stress you're dealing with at home and go have some fun with your friends.

9.5 But Can They Still Come Over?

Before cancer, you might have had friends over after school—study dates, sleepovers, or parties. Now your home may not be the ideal place for friend gatherings.

Your parent might be conked out on the couch after a chemo treatment. Your parent might have lost their hair.

Surgery may have left scars. Plus, the mood at your house may be tense, filled with a bit more stress or sadness than usual.

Should your house become a no-friend zone? Not necessarily.

You might talk to your parents and siblings and make a policy about having friends over. Is everyone okay with it? Are certain days taboo (right after a chemo treatment) or certain times off-limits (late night if your family wants it quiet in the house)? Are certain rooms off limits? Maybe your mom wants to claim the TV room when she's feeling sick. Or maybe your parents would rather not have anyone upstairs. Your family might decide on other policies like:

- Ask before having a friend over.
- Invite only one or two people over at a time (instead of a larger group).
- Invite only close friends (not unfamiliar faces).
- Limit activities: maybe watching a movie or doing homework together is fine, but blasting loud music is not.

Even if it is totally fine with your family, you still might not want to have friends over. That is totally fine. So you don't seem rude you can let the friends know this when you tell them about your parent's cancer. Just add something like, "Oh, and hey, guys, I think I probably won't have people over while my family is dealing with this. Is it okay if we just hang at your places or go out instead of coming to my house?"

If you want to give them a reason, explain that things are "kind of crazy" at home or that you want to get out of the house as much as possible or just blame it on your parents, as in "they don't want me having people over."

Marc says: Don't worry, parents are usually happy to play the bad guy!

9.6 Social Networks: Facebook, Twitter, Blogs, and More

Should you go digital with facts (and feelings) about your parent's cancer? That's your call. But there's a lot to think about before you do.

9.6.1 How It Can Help

Some teens keep friends up to date via social media sites like Facebook or blogs or texts or email. That can be easier than making lots of calls to let people know about a parent's diagnosis or a change in condition. Even if you just text one friend, the message will spread. Sometimes that can be a relief—you don't have to contact everyone in your circle, but they will get the word and rally around you to offer support.

"When I first found out, I called a few friends and kept it quiet for a while out of respect for my dad," remembers a fifteen-year-old girl whose father has been fighting cancer for a year. "I then used Facebook to inform the rest of my friends what exactly was going on. The support from my friends via Facebook was very helpful."

You may also find that blogging is helpful. "I had a blog where I would very, very occasionally allude to things about my mom's health," one teen says. "I wasn't so great at talking to people about how I felt. I often felt pressured to do so and incompetent when I couldn't verbalize it properly. So in a place like a blog, I had control over what I put out there."

You may come across a Facebook page or online message board just for teens (or kids) coping with a parent's cancer. (See the Resources in Appendix D.) That can be kind of a safe digital space—your school friends won't read what you post. People in a similar situation might read your comments and perhaps offer useful advice.

9.6.2 WHY YOU MIGHT BE WARY OF SOCIAL MEDIA

Lots of kids make a decision to keep cancer out of their digital communications. Just as teens often prefer to keep a low profile about their mom's or dad's cancer at school, they don't want to be known on Facebook as the Kid Whose Parent Has Cancer.

And make no mistake: whatever you post on Facebook is tattooed on your digital forehead. Acquaintances with a cruel streak might tease you or make comments like, "You think you've got problems, listen to what's going on with me..." And that will only make you feel worse.

If you do decide to use Facebook to talk about your parent's cancer, check first with Mom or Dad, or both. They may not have told, say, a boss at work or certain friends. And in that case, your Facebook post could make life awkward for them.

9.6.3 TRUE DIGITAL CONFESSIONS

Another kind of Facebook posting takes place. Some teens don't use the word "cancer" but put up comments that clearly allude to their parent's situation. Like: "Having a really tough time, girlfriend broke up with me, dad is sick." Or "I don't know if I can take this anymore, between taking care of my sick mom and trying to pass my finals."

At times teens will also post vague messages that might indicate suicidal thoughts or experimenting with behaviors like cutting or anorexia: "I tried something that other kids at school do when they're feeling down. It didn't make me feel any better..."

Why put such private thoughts in a public space? You know everyone will read what you write. Yet when you sit and write a post at your keyboard, you may feel anonymous.

9.7 Dealing with Friend Problems

It's one thing when a friend says the wrong thing or isn't quite sure how to act. It's another when they turn their back on you, spread rumors, or commit some other very-not-cool violation of your friendship.

Friends can get you through your parent's cancer or add more stress to your life. And you're not the only one who might have annoying friends.

Some friends might not know how to handle the news that your parent has cancer. One girl remembers that a friend accused her of making up the story about her mom's cancer just to get attention. Sheesh!

And there will probably be a few friends who react by distancing themselves from you. Try not to let that get you down.

Words of Wisdom:

If someone is teasing you about a parent's chemo-baldness and you feel compelled to say something, social worker Barbara Golby suggests: "Be neutral and brief and direct." You might say: "My mom has cancer. She's getting medicine that makes her hair fall out and that's why she's bald." Then walk away and be done with it.

"When I told my friends," remembers Tyler T., fourteen, of Utah, "we'd already started hanging out together less because their personalities were changing to stuff that I knew was wrong. So when I told them, they started pulling away even more. I had only one friend in the whole school. That was really hard. But I did have a bunch of friends in my [church congregation], and the people that probably helped me the most were my scout leaders and my other youth leaders."

· ·

When Friends Cross the Line

Once in a while, people will say something mean. We're talking *really* mean.

Rachel of New York, whose mom died of breast cancer, remembers a so-called friend telling "your momma" jokes to her—like "Knock, knock. Who's there? Not your momma." And saying "Oh, sorry." But to Rachel, "it wasn't a heartfelt sorry."

Abby, her campmate at Camp Kesem, the camp for kids coping with a parent's cancer, gave this advice: "I would never talk to that person again. Tell them to keep that person away."

Paul G. of Ohio was on the hockey team when his mom was going through cancer treatment. Another kid on the team would tease him about his mom. He can't remember exactly what his teammate said. "Something about her baldness," Paul says. "I was totally annoyed. I had a horrible season, and I almost quit." And the kid teasing him was the coach's son.

Isn't cancer a line you don't cross? "The answer is, it would be nice, but it isn't," says psychiatrist Paula Rauch. This is a time when having a go-to grown-up can be a big help. You can share the dilemma and then talk it out—do you want to ignore the issue, wait for it to run its course, or talk to an authority figure?

Some kids would rather just let it be. Others want to figure out what to say. You don't want to spring into action without a plan. If you consult an adult, the two of you can come up with a plan. Maybe you and your parent would want to approach a school counselor or social worker. Maybe, in Paul's case, you might want to ask the counselor about scheduling a session with the whole soccer team to discuss what coping with a parent's cancer is like.

Paul didn't do that, but he did come up with his own theory about what happened. He thinks the coach's son ragged on him because Paul was getting a lot of attention from teammates who were concerned about his mom. In certain circumstances, understanding why something happens is enough.

As for Rachel, she posted a note on her Facebook page aimed at the mean girl who made "your momma jokes," something like: "My mom just died. Can you give me a break?" Everyone figured out who Rachel was talking about—including the girl who told the jokes. She told Rachel: "You made me look like a jerk on Facebook." Looking back, Rachel regrets going public.

• •

• •

Emily's Story: "Teenagers Are Jerks"
Emily's mom was diagnosed with breast cancer when Emily was fourteen, which she describes as "already kind of a tumultuous time when you're kind of an ass-hole…" Emily was angry at the cancer for striking her mom and angry at her mom for getting sick.

And she was especially angry at one of her best friends.

Emily told her friend, "I'm so scared. My mom is sick." She went into details about how she was feeling.

The next day in homeroom, this friend gave Emily a long, handwritten note. Emily remembers reading, "I'm the lead in the play right now and I can't handle my friend's mother having cancer. There's too much on my plate."

Emily says, "The gist of it was she couldn't be my friend because she couldn't handle my mother having cancer. It was like a huge hit in the stomach."

Not only did Emily lose that friend, but some of Emily's other friends abandoned her to hang out with the Girl Who Rejected Emily. All Emily was left with was her good friend Robinson. "Robinson just treated me like everything was normal." And that's exactly what Emily needed.

• •

Hard times will often weed out the good friends from the bad. If your "friends" pull away or tell you they can't hang out anymore, they're not your real friends.

Alternatively, you might pull away from your friends. Katie of Washington, who lost her dad to stomach cancer, was seventeen when he was diagnosed and a senior in high school. "I probably dealt with it pretty badly," she says. One of her best friends was super sensitive, always asking, "Is he okay? Are you okay?"

"I pushed her away," Katie says. "A couple of friends were pretty unemotional, and I spent most of my time with [them]. As her dad grew sicker with stomach cancer, Katie remembers, "I very selfishly decided to deal with my own grief by pushing it away, going out with friends, [not] spending more time at home."

Worst Thing I Heard:

When Callie's mom was diagnosed with pancreatic cancer, her friends said the *wrong* thing: "I have never heard of anyone surviving pancreatic cancer," and "Wow, don't people usually die really fast after they find out they have pancreatic cancer?" "These were said without a thought to my feelings or how it would affect me," says Callie, whose mother is today a ten-year survivor.

"There's a lot worse things people go through," is what Ellen, sixteen, remembers hearing as both her parents fought cancer—and survived.

"It's not a big deal" is what one friend told Vanessa, whose dad was diagnosed with liver cancer when she was fifteen and died two years later. "It's such a casual statement," Vanessa says, "and yet incredibly insensitive and hurtful. Yet I believe someone says something like that because they are ignorant and they have no idea what it means to watch someone they love suffer while there is nothing they can do to help."

9.8 New Friends

Maybe you just moved and are making new buddies. Or you might just be in a time of transition, moving from one set of friends to another. You might hesitate about telling these new friends. They hardly know you. How will they react?

> "I was in school trying to make new friends. There were people I was becoming good friends with that maybe I would want to have over. I don't think I told many of them. I was trying to fit in. I didn't want to be that kid that had something going on at home."
> —Alison S., whose family moved from Portland to Seattle
> just before her mom was diagnosed with breast cancer

If you're a teen who's just starting college when your parent is diagnosed, you will invariably deal with new friends. Don Fisher's daughter Jennifer was seventeen when her mother died of cancer. Jennifer found great support from her new friends and a new boyfriend during her freshman year at the University of Chicago. "That support meant all the world to her," says Don.

chapter 10

School Daze

School is where it all goes down. It's what you do most every day. It's your J-O-B. It's where you learn stuff (and stress out about not learning enough stuff to get the grades you want), hang out in the halls, torment teachers, play sports, act in the school play, get involved in student government, and much more. As you try to excel in whatever ways are important to you, a parent's cancer can seem like a major interruption.

This chapter will address school from two angles:

1. **Keeping up:** How to keep up with work, maintain grades, and communicate with teachers.
2. **Keeping cool:** How to do the cool stuff that lets you express yourself and enjoy yourself.

10.1 School = More Stress or a Place to Escape?

Life is busy and stressful enough. Fitting in is a challenge in itself. And school isn't exactly a picnic. Then Mom or Dad is diagnosed with cancer.

How are you supposed to handle it all?

On the one hand, school can be a good thing, a place you can go to get away from cancer and the stress it causes at home. Child life specialist Sandi Ring talks about how school can help keep things together: "It's the normalcy—a reminder that life does go on, and I think it's important to encourage kids that you will be going to school. This is your responsibility."

On the other hand, you may feel like your whole world has come crashing down, that everything is different. How do you go to school and act as if nothing has changed?

> "If anything, school was just a really good distraction. It wasn't the best distraction, but it was always there."
> —Stephanie, fourteen, of Utah

> "My mom didn't make us feel bad for being wrapped up in our high-school and middle-school lives. She's a very strong person. She kept our lives as normal as possible."
> —Alison S. of Washington, whose mom is a breast cancer survivor

> "Going to school every day normalized my life. I could put cancer to the back of my mind for a little while."
> —Samantha, who was seventeen when her mother was diagnosed with cancer

10.2 To Announce or Not to Announce

How much do you want the word to get out at school? Do you want to keep it private? We'll discuss how you communicate with teachers, counselors, administrators, and other staffers in this chapter. (Sharing with friends is covered in Chapter 9.)

At one boy's middle school in Texas, the administrators learned that the boy's mom had cancer. And they announced the news over the PA system to the entire school! The school meant well. But...wow. "The student was a little bit horrified," says the social worker who told us the story. Probably more than a little bit!

We hope nothing like that happens to you—the sharing of intimate information without your permission. But you do have to think about the Big Questions: whom do we tell and how do we tell them? Because this is a decision that involves both you and your parents, the next few sections of this chapter are aimed at you, as well as your parents.

First, let's talk about you. Maybe you think you don't have to tell anybody at school. And maybe you'll be fine. Maybe you'll work extra hard to keep your grades up so your parents will be proud of you. Or maybe you just feel good when you're getting A's.

Then again, maybe you'll be like Kaitlin, fifteen, after her mom was diagnosed with Stage 4 breast cancer: "During treatment I didn't care about school. I couldn't care less, and I didn't study. I did homework but not to my fullest ability. I didn't care to sit in class and focus on things not important to me. I had other things on my mind, how she was doing."

Or like Tyler R. of Virginia: "It wasn't in school that I had a problem. It was after I got home. It was just hard studying, and that translated into bad grades on quizzes and tests." Part of the reason is that he was trying to do more around the house to help out after his dad's cancer diagnosis.

And it's not just your academic chops that might change. Travis B. of Manitoba notes that many teens feel "alienated at their schools. They felt alone, almost."

So no matter how much you might think: "Don't tell the school," every expert we interviewed said it's usually a "good practice" to tell the school.

If you're feeling distracted or upset, if your grades are slipping, the school will understand why if people there know what's happening. Instead of giving you grief, the school may be able to give you support. If you feel the need to talk, you will have someone to talk to who knows what's going on.

Still you beg your parents: don't tell. And your parents

might end up coming around to your point of view. Why raise a stink when nothing's wrong? And maybe, even though we just said it's good to tell, it might be okay not to tell in your case...but only *if* your parent has an early stage cancer and treatment is pretty straightforward, and if you and your parents are talking about how things are going on a regular basis.

Even if you are in the "don't tell" camp, you might consider a slight compromise. Tell one person on the school staff and swear that person to secrecy, proposes social worker Seth Berkowitz. At least that way you have someone to go to if anything should change at home and the school needs to know.

Remember: Telling the school doesn't have to mean an announcement over the PA. It doesn't mean your teachers will each tell the class, "John's dad has cancer."

You and your parents can talk about whom to inform, and what the guidelines are, and how private or public the information is. Sit down and have a conversation about how to deal with school in a way that's comfortable for you. Come to an agreement that you all can live with.

10.3 Telling the School

> "I told my teachers, 'I just want you to know as a heads-up that my father has cancer. I don't know if it's going to get worse or not. I'm not asking for extra time for assignments. I just want you to know in case things get worse and I may need some leeway.'"
>
> —Marlene of Washington, whose dad was
> diagnosed with cancer when she was fourteen

Since you spend so much time at school, you may want to find avenues of support. That way, if you have a rough moment and need someone to talk to, you'll know where to turn. Plus, if you're having difficulty balancing school with your parent's cancer, you'll have a sympathetic adult who can help you work through it. "He became a really good friend to me," Bailee recalls, remembering the conversations she had with her guidance counselor when her mom was being treated for breast cancer.

At your school, someone among the people listed below might become a good go-to person. Approach the individual and ask if you can come to talk from time to time. Or you might want to set up a regular check-in.

Words of Wisdom:
"It's crucial that the teacher know what's going on," says child life specialist Sandi Ring. "Any educator who's going to be in contact with the child on a daily basis needs to have an awareness and sensitivity toward what's going on."

- **School social worker or psychologist.** See if you can set up a meeting and ask if you can talk in the future on an as-needed basis.
- **Guidance counselor.** If you've got a good relationship with your counselor, this may be the time to go a little deeper in your conversations.
- **Trusted teacher or coach.** If you have a strong relationship with a teacher, present or past, ask if the teacher might be available to talk if you run into any classroom problems or other issues.
- **School nurse.** No, the nurse isn't just for runny noses and skinned knees. The nurse might be able to help you sort out cancer issues as well as providing medical information and a sympathetic ear.

10.4 HOW THE SCHOOL CAN HELP

Check in with you. The counselor (or another mentor-type figure) can check in with you weekly or so to see how things are going, grade-wise and otherwise. Maybe you forgot to do one or two assignments. Maybe everything is fine. Or you might welcome the chance to unburden your thoughts to someone: "This was a tough week. I can't stand seeing my mom going through this."

Check in with your parents. The counselor can also touch base with your parents weekly or at another frequency to share good updates, as well as any changes in grades or classroom behavior that are cause for concern.

The subtle signal. You might talk to your teacher about establishing a signal that means: "I'm having a rough moment. I don't need to leave class, but please don't call on me right now." It could be as simple as catching the teacher's eye and flashing a thumbs-down.

The "leaving class" pass. Some schools issue a pass to kids coping with a parent's illness, good for a ten- or fifteen-minute break or maybe for the duration of the class. No questions asked. Show the pass, get out of class. The student might just go to the bathroom, wash his or her face, take a deep breath, then return to class. Or the arrangement might be that the student will go to the guidance counselor's office, either to talk to someone or just to hang out in the waiting area. Maybe you'll say to the counselor, "I'm having a bad day." If you and the counselor are close, maybe you'll get a hug. And then you'll head back to class, better able to cope.

Survival Tip: The pass is something to use, not to abuse. If you take too much advantage of the pass, it might be confiscated. Use it when you need it, not when you're bored in class.

• •

Paul's Story: A Helpful Pass

Paul's mom, Janis, who was diagnosed with breast cancer, took the initiative to go talk to his school without telling him first. But he was okay with it.

Janis: "I had meetings with Paul's teachers and guidance counselor."

Paul: "She just did it. That was fine with me. Overall teachers were supportive. If I missed school to be home with my mom, they gave me work to make up and didn't yell at me.

"I had an emergency pass. If I was upset, I didn't have to ask or explain. I'd just use the pass and go to the guidance counselor. I tried to get my mom's cancer to the back of my head but sometimes it distracted me. That's when I used my pass."

• •

10.5 DILEMMAS, DILEMMAS

Even with the best lines of communication, glitches will occur. Here are three case histories—and possible solutions:

Dilemma: "The teacher called on me and said, 'Oh, how's your mom doing?' It's a science class. I didn't like it." Kaitlin wanted to answer the question about science, not deliver a medical bulletin.

Solution: Try not to be too angry at your intrusive teacher, says school psychologist Ricia Weiner. The teacher probably meant well. It's just that "teachers don't have training the way [mental health professionals] do in dealing with sensitive matters." You or your parent might go to the teacher and say, "We appreciate your concern, but please don't ask about the cancer situation during class." Asking after class, in private, might be an alternative. Kaitlin says she wouldn't have minded that.

Dilemma: Marlene's dad was diagnosed with cancer. Her mom told one of Marlene's teachers at parent night. The next day, the teacher led a very strange discussion.

He asked the class: if your parent had cancer and there was a drug that you couldn't afford to treat the cancer, would you steal it? His goal, he said, was to talk about the Machiavellian principle: when does the just become unjust and the unjust become just?

He singled Marlene out several times, including in this horrifying tale: "Let's say an attacker breaks into the room, puts a gun in Marlene's hand, and says, 'I want you to shoot Kyle, and if you do, the rest of the class lives.'"

He also told the class that pretty much all of them would develop cancer if they live long enough.

"I came home and started crying," Marlene remembers. "I don't know what to think about this."

Solution: Marlene's mom knew what to think about it. She went to school and had Marlene transferred into another class.

Dilemma: Lyndsey's mom has breast cancer that's spread to other organs. Lyndsey plays a big role in helping out at home with younger siblings and keeps her grades up at school. But one day she forgot to do homework for one subject. Lyndsey says: "The teacher pulled me out and asked, 'Do you have time to do homework?' He tried to make it all about my mom having cancer, and I was *freaking out* because I really just forgot to do it."

Solution: Let the teacher know, perhaps with the help of a guidance counselor or your parent, that it's not right to play the cancer card for every little problem. Maybe Lyndsey really did forget because her mom has cancer. And the teacher's comment just reminded Lyndsey of how much it sucks when your mom has cancer. But maybe Lyndsey just forgot. Period. What Lyndsey really wants—what many teens want—is for the teacher to treat her as he always does.

10.6 Keeping Grades Up

What if you're falling behind? Missed some classes and haven't got the class notes yet. Running late on homework because last night Dad had to go to the hospital or because Mom has been hospitalized for weeks and you visit every day after school.

Or your chore load at home has increased.

> "I let my grades slip down, and I'm not proud of that because I should've just kept up with [schoolwork]."
>
> —Allison B., thirteen, of Idaho

> "When my dad was diagnosed, my grades went in the toilet."
>
> —Reilly, sixteen, of Virginia

If grades are slowly slipping into the danger zone, you and your parents can ask the school for help. No school will say, "Forget about it. Parental cancer equals an Automatic A." But with the aid of your school social worker or counselor, you can negotiate:

1. **Later deadlines or makeup tests.** That might be helpful for one project. Extending all your deadlines has a downside, notes social worker Seth Berkowitz. You'll never catch up with the next round of work. Another option, he suggests: turn the project in on time and ask if the teacher can consider your circumstances in assigning a grade.

2. **Shorter assignments.** Parent and counselor (or student and counselor) can talk to certain teachers about modifying homework. Is it okay to do just half the assigned math problems? Can a research project be five pages instead of ten? These kinds of adjustments might be helpful if things aren't going so well on the cancer front.

Your parents might be your advocate. School psychologist Ricia Weiner suggests that the parents let the child's counselor know that the child is struggling to keep up with schoolwork and ask if the counselor can send a message to the teachers along these lines: "Please boil down assignments to those that are most essential for content knowledge. Please be considerate of the student and family at this point in time. We will keep you posted."

Words of Wisdom:

"What a teacher should say is, 'If you need something, I'm here after school. Just come by.'"

—Social worker Seth Berkowitz

If you explain that you're doing homework while visiting your dad in the hospital every day after school or between making dinner and packing lunches for younger siblings each night, the teacher might say, "Wow, that would be tough for me if I were in your shoes."

Survival Tip: If you find yourself struggling to get help with homework and studying and your parents are too busy to help, where do you turn?

- There's strength in numbers. Ask your friends if you can study or work with them at their house so their parents can help out with challenging questions.

- Ask a teacher if you can stay after school for a bit to go over confusing concepts.

- Ask a family friend or relative (especially one who lives close by) if they could help you with a challenging assignment.

- Many schools have peer tutors—go see one! Or if it's in the family budget, see if your parents might be able to hire a tutor to help you through a difficult patch.

10.7 THE NEED TO ACHIEVE

On the opposite side of the spectrum are the teens who pour themselves into school, who aim to excel. That's how some teens react to intense stress, including a parent's cancer. They become overachievers.

"They don't cause trouble. They fly under the radar," explains child life specialist Sandi Ring. And then you seem like you're doing great. So no one pays attention to *your* needs, including your parents.

It's okay to give yourself a break. And it'd be really nice if your parents could tell you how proud they are of you...but also let you know that it's okay not to be perfect.

> "It's school I regret spending so much time on. I got great grades but I didn't build friendships through the grades. It was just getting good grades because I could. I did enjoy some of the subjects. I tried to get an A in everything, but I didn't enjoy everything.
>
> —Jenny of Massachusetts, whose mother died of cancer

10.7.1 WHERE TO CUT BACK, WHERE TO RAMP UP

Debate team, soccer, student government, plays, yearbook, oh my! Not everyone fills up their schedules with a million extracurriculars—clubs, activities, and sports—but many teens have that drive to stay busy. Maybe they just like it. Or maybe they hope that their wide range of activities will help create an impressive college application.

If you've got a full plate, you may decide that something's got to give after your parent is diagnosed with cancer. You will have more pressures on your time and your mind. It's possible you might become overwhelmed. If your activities provide a welcome outlet for stress and aren't getting in the way of anything, by all means keep them! If you find yourself stretched too thin, consider dropping an activity or two. Or try talking to the teacher or adviser or student club sponsor about cutting back for a spell until things settle down at home.

If you consider cutting an activity from your repertoire, keep the ones that reduce your stress level and make you happy. Keep the ones that don't require extra work once you get home. Ditch the ones that cause more stress or eat up too much of your precious time.

10.8 Pulling a Bueller

Don't make a habit of using your parent's cancer as an excuse to stay home from school. But every now and then you might need a day off. Here are three good reasons to follow in the footsteps of filmdom's famous school skipper, Ferris Bueller:

Words of Wisdom:

"If you really want to be with your parent instead of at school, that might be the very best thing for you! Your ability to focus in school is going to be impacted. And you'll have some one-on-one time with Mom or Dad. Those stolen moments will really mean a lot."

—Child life specialist Sandi Ring

1. **A big treatment day:** Your parent is having a treatment or surgical procedure, and you want to be there for them at the hospital.

2. **Mental health day:** You need a breather to collect your thoughts and emotions or want to avoid breaking down at school.

3. **Things are getting worse:** Your parent's prognosis is not good, and you want to spend as much time as possible with your parent while you have the chance.

chapter 11

SEEKING SUPPORT

Perhaps your family and friends are giving you the support you need to cope. Or maybe you're the kind of person who figures out by yourself what you need to do to cope. (For more on that, see Chapter 6.)

Or maybe you'd benefit by talking with someone who's not your mom, dad, sibling, or best friend. That person might be an adult who's been there for you in the past—an aunt or uncle or grandparent, a teacher, a school counselor, a minister, a coach, a friend's parent. Then again, you might be the kind of teen who benefits from a support group or by meeting with a therapist. This chapter will look at different sources of outside support.

> "You don't have to go through it alone; you don't have to put on this defense. Looking back, I think I really would have liked to find a support system, to have somebody to talk to who knew what was going on. Don't keep it to yourself. Try to find someone you feel will help you get your emotions out."
>
> —Erin of Florida, whose dad was diagnosed with lung cancer when she was sixteen and died a year later

> "Keep a positive attitude and give much love to your parent. Educate yourself and talk to others. Don't be embarrassed to

reach out to friends, relatives, and other adults. Check into online groups of teens dealing with the same issues. When I was dealing with this, there were none of these things, and my parents did not want to talk about it."

—Sandy, whose mother was diagnosed with breast cancer when she was three and died when Sandy was twenty-three

Head Count: Did you have an adult that helped you through your parent's cancer?

- 52% said yes
- 49% said no

11.1 The Adult Who Knows You

Now may be the time to run through your mental list of adults in your life. Is there one grown-up who's been your confidant and supporter in the past? Maybe an aunt or uncle or really cool cousin or a favorite teacher, coach, or counselor at school. Maybe even a friend's parent. When you find that person, you'll know. They'll listen to what you have to say and offer the kind of verbal support you need.

"The kind of person you want to be able to talk to is one who is basically a positive person but not a simple-minded smiley face," notes psychiatrist James Gordon. "That's not helpful."

Your parents might be helpful in figuring out who the person is. You might even talk with them about how to pick your go-to adult. It might be Aunt Joanie or Uncle David or your best friend's mom. That way, you'll have someone to talk to if you have any questions or concerns and don't want to burden your mom or dad (or if they're not around because of doctor's visits and the like).

A grandparent can also be a wonderful confidant. "My

grandpa made it feel like nothing [bad] was going to happen and that everything was going to be okay," says Austen, fifteen, who was ten when his dad was diagnosed with leukemia. "He'd take me fishing and we'd talk about it a lot. That helped—just to talk about it and have fun with your grandpa."

And when you have a confidant like that, you're less likely to feel lonely. A study of 221 teens who had a parent with cancer found that about one in ten experienced loneliness. And sometimes the problem was that they didn't have friends they could really talk about matters with.

"I wish I had someone close to my age that I could tell," says Morgan of Seattle, whose dad was diagnosed with cancer when she was fifteen and died when she was sixteen. "In my peers, no one ever had to deal with anything I had to deal with. I didn't have anyone to connect with on that level."

Looking back with seven years of perspective, she says, "I handled my dad's cancer the only way I knew how at the time. I wish I would have tried to be more open with other people. It would have been really helpful if I weren't so closed off."

Morgan still gets "choked up" thinking about her father. "That will never go away," she says, "But I've learned that talking it out with someone really does help."

• •

Bailee's Story: Finding a Confidant

When Bailee was twelve, her mom faced cancer. Bailee had three younger sisters, ages one, four, and six at the time. Bailee says, "My real dad wasn't really ever a part of my life." And her stepdad had a job in California, so he spent more time working there than he did on the home front in Medicine Hat, a town in Alberta, Canada.

"I did feel responsible," says Bailee. "It was hard. When you're twelve, you have nothing on your mind but friends and school. It was kind of like the mother role got laid on me."

One thing that helped a lot was having someone to talk to—a school counselor she was close to. "He just really reassured me that even though it sucked for the time being and my social life got cut off, that I was doing the right thing. I was the bigger person for stepping up and being with my family when they needed me instead of just saying, 'Oh, it's going to be okay.'

"I didn't want to overwhelm my mom with questions—and there were just so many questions. With my counselor, I know he cared but he could answer my questions and listen to them and let me talk. He became one of my best friends, my biggest rock I could ever talk to."

Bailee's experience echoes what many studies have found—that for kids in tough circumstances, having a mentor, a confidant, an adult who provides support, is what helps them to thrive despite all odds.

• •

11.2 Seeing a Therapist

That doesn't mean it's easy to summon the courage to ask for help.

First off, don't worry what people will think of you. Consider the advice of psychiatrist Paula Rauch: if you think you'd benefit by having someone to talk to, you're making "a strong, healthy decision." Like Bailee, you may turn to your school counselor. Or maybe you're more comfortable with a favorite teacher, a coach, your pediatrician, a pastor you know.

Then there's the "t" word—therapist. (See sidebar on page

146 to learn what a therapy session is like.) Your pediatrician or guidance counselor, or a local cancer center, might be able to recommend someone.

"Don't be afraid to go see a therapist. Dude, it can only help."
—Reilly, sixteen, who says his therapist helped him understand
why he did some of the not-so-good things he did as
a way to fill the hole in his soul after his father died

"It was really helpful to have someone to talk to, without any judgment."
—Hakeem, sixteen, who saw a school therapist once a
week when his dad was dealing with pancreatic cancer

Some questions to think about if you're interested, courtesy of Elissa Bantug, the former teen rebel (her story is in Chapter 7) who now counsels cancer patients:

- Would you prefer a male or female?
- Is there a time that works for you and won't mess up your other commitments? Saturday morning? After school? Evening?
- Are you willing to give it a try for, say, three visits before deciding if the therapist is helpful for you? (And if your decision is that the therapist is not helpful, Bantug suggests you tell your parents, who "should respect" your conclusion.)

As for the issue of paying for therapy: many communities have mental health clinics that will work with your family to make therapy affordable. The Cancer Support Community, a national group with many local chapters, offers no-cost options as do other cancer support groups. The Resources section of the book also can refer you to several groups that will connect you with a social worker for a phone conversation.

· ·

What's It Like to See a Therapist?

Social work professor Victoria Rizzo offers a guide to the world of therapy.

Does this mean I'm crazy?

"It's just another person to talk to. It doesn't mean anyone thinks something's wrong with you."

Do I have to go?

"Go in and meet the person and talk with them. If you don't think the person is right for you or not helping, you don't have to do it anymore."

Will I be judged?

"A therapist is someone you can talk to who can be more objective, who is not going to judge you, who is not going to side with certain people in the family. You can say whatever you need to and you won't be judged."

In ten words or less, what is a therapist like?

"A therapist is like a really good, nonjudgmental parent."

· ·

11.3 Group Support

In some areas of the country, support groups are available specifically to help teenagers who have a parent with cancer. Let's say there's a group in your area. Would you consider going?

Not everyone would be interested, and that's fine. We're not all the support group type.

But unlike your friends at school, the kids you meet in support groups are all going through similar experiences. They will instantly get what you're going through.

You can also gain some perspective. "It made you realize you weren't the only one in the whole world going through the same struggles," recalls Tyler R., who went to Camp Kesem, a camp for kids who are dealing with a parent's cancer. "Honestly, I had it easy compared to other kids at camp." Tyler's dad had a tough time during treatment for an "aggressive" lymphoma, but today he is in good health.

For some teens, a support group is a great place to share their story with people going through similar experiences. The teenagers don't always come eagerly. *My mom brought me here. I didn't want to get out of the car.* That's what teens tell Suzanne Brace, executive director of Baltimore's HopeWell Cancer Support, which offers Teen Circle.

Once the teens do get out of the car, they're often glad they did. Many of the teens we interviewed found a lot of comfort and value in a support group.

> "It was really good to know they were going through the same stuff that I was. They did have a bit better insight because they were going through it or had been through it."
> —Alex about Kids Can Cope, the support group offered by CancerCare Manitoba that he attended in Winnipeg when he was fourteen and his mother was being treated for breast cancer

> "I'm a guy. It's hard for me to talk about it. That was the good thing about the support group. They never pressured you into talking at all. It helped me realize I wasn't alone, you know, that there were other people going through the same thing I was. Some unfortunately even worse."
> —Travis B. of Manitoba, another Kids Can Cope member

MY PARENT HAS CANCER AND IT REALLY SUCKS

11.3.1 So, What's a Support Group Like Anyway?

There aren't a ton of support groups out there for teens whose parents have cancer. Teens aren't exactly demanding them. Schedules are busy with school activities and homework. And when a parent has cancer, teens face more demands on the home front.

But groups do exist—in Baltimore, Cleveland, Houston, and Tucson, to name a few locations.

Usually a cancer support organization or hospital specializing in cancer will run the groups. (Check out the Resources section in Appendix D for info.) Some of the groups are specifically for teens who've lost a parent to cancer. (We'll cover that type of group in Chapter 13.) Other groups are open to anyone coping with a parent's cancer.

The groups may meet weekly, every two weeks, or monthly. Sometimes they have a time limit—say, once a week for six weeks. The group leader is typically a social worker or other mental health professional who has worked with families facing a parent's cancer and has counseled teens over the years.

In case you're curious, here's what goes on at some of these groups:

Food. Either dinner or snacks, drawn from the staples of the teen diet: pizza, chicken wings, chips, cookies, soda.

Cancer class. One session is usually devoted to discussing the disease itself. A guest speaker or a PowerPoint presentation from the group leader will cover the nature of cancer, the symptoms, the treatments. Questions are welcome.

Open discussion. That's part of pretty much every group. Maybe the group leader will toss out a word to trigger talk that week—sad, confused, happy. Or maybe the teens will just get into it on their own—Mom had a bad week; Dad got good news. Whatever's on your mind can come out.

148

Activities: express yourself! You might think: *I am too old for projects.* Or a particular project might not be your thing. When a group leader asked the teens to color in a shield and write the words that represent how they protect themselves, Reilly, sixteen, who lost his dad to cancer, said, "You know I don't like coloring." On the other hand, you might really get into it and find that it's easier to talk while you're doing something. Reilly ends up saying, "I wrote a word, and I'm going to color it. Boom, look at that: Courage."

Action. Balloons are big. Group members may write all the things about cancer that make them angry on a big poster board, then toss water balloons at the board. The splat, we hear, is very satisfying. Or they may write their hopes for their parent on a slip of paper, put the paper inside a balloon, and send the balloon off into the heavens.

Homework. Blurgh, you do not want more homework! But some groups suggest that participants keep a journal and will even give questions to address. For groups with a limited run, kids may share entries from their journals at the final session.

• •

How to Start Your Own Support Group

Kelly Schwab's mom was diagnosed with breast cancer the summer before Kelly's junior year in high school. "My mind immediately went to the worst." Kelly remembers thinking: "What is life going to be like without my mom?"

Kelly's mom had a good prognosis. She had a mastectomy and did not need to undergo chemotherapy or radiation. That was a huge relief for the family. But Kelly didn't just put cancer in the past. "I realized there weren't resources for teens," she says. "You can talk to your friends and everything, but they don't know what a diagnosis does to a family, even if you have a good prognosis."

149

She approached the Claudia Mayer Cancer Resource Center (CMRC) to start a support group in Columbia, Maryland, where the Schwab family lives. Two other teens in the area also approached the center with the same idea. CMRC worked with the Ulman Cancer Fund for Young Adults to set up the group. And Teens Together was born.

At monthly meetings, a CMRC social worker is there to keep the conversation flowing and address issues that come up. "Sometimes we just talk about normal life," says Kelly. "Sometimes the conversation goes to people not understanding what's going on. And sometimes we talk about the crazy stuff our parents do, like crazy diets." For her, the group has been a way of reaching out to help other people "even if you have tough stuff going on in your own life." She adds: "You probably end up helping yourself, too."

Chapter 12

FACING A DIRE PROGNOSIS

The news that a parent has cancer is hard enough to cope with. It's a million times harder when the prognosis is gloomy. When the cancer is hard to treat or has spread beyond its original site. When doctors aren't sure if they can beat the cancer into remission. When doctors think the patient has a limited amount of time to live—maybe a year, maybe just months.

It's what no patient wants to hear. And it's devastating for the family as well. But there are different kinds of dire prognoses. And in all cases, hope is part of the picture.

12.1 FACING THE NEWS

"Even though I know my mom only has two years to live, it hurts when other people tell you, 'That's life. We all live and die.' You can't help but feel as though they're downplaying the seriousness of the disease."

—Samantha, twenty, whose mom was diagnosed
with breast cancer three years ago

• •

Travis's Story: Hoping for Disney World
Travis W.'s dad got some news. It wasn't good news. Dad had cancer. A kind called multiple myeloma.

Travis had never heard of multiple myeloma. (That's not so surprising. There are only about 21,700 new cases a year for what the American Cancer Society calls a "relatively uncommon" cancer found in white blood cells in the bone marrow. Multiple myeloma can lie quiet for a long time. It can respond to treatment. Or it can be very aggressive.)

"I have been given six months to live," Travis's dad told his kids.

Travis had no trouble understanding "the six months part." He said, "Oh no!"

And his upbeat dad said, "Who wants to go to Disney World?"

"So I'm like, 'Uh, okay,'" Travis says. "Yes, sure, let's go to Disney World!"

But in the back of Travis's mind was the question: "When is it going to happen?"

12.2 How Long Do We Have?

When is it going to happen? Even though doctors can give a range for survival, they can't give a precise prediction. Sometimes a patient can outlive a doctor's prediction by months, even years. Someone in good health might be able to fight a little longer. Chemotherapy might keep the cancer in check. Maybe a new drug treatment will come along, perhaps in a clinical trial, that will make a difference.

"It is important to know there are outliers, exceptional survivors," says oncologist Lidia Schapira.

Your parent can hope to be one of the patients who does better than anyone could have expected. You can hope for that, too. "Almost everybody still hopes for a miracle up until the last breath," says Mae Greenberg, a mental health counselor who leads bereavement groups for the Cancer Support Community in Miami.

As for Travis's dad, he defied everyone's predictions. Ten years after his death sentence, he is still alive. And fighting.

12.3 WHEN THE BAD NEWS ISN'T ALL BAD

If the diagnosis is metastatic disease—cancer that has spread from its primary site to other organs—that's a cause for worry. But even a patient with metastatic disease might have a number of years ahead. In some cases, treatments can keep the cancer in check.

You might wonder: how do I act around Mom or Dad? And how will Mom or Dad treat me?

Words of Wisdom:

"For every type and stage of cancer, there is an average of how long the patient might live, based on statistics. We can give a range and do so quite accurately. What we can say is that if the cancer is terminal, 50 percent of patients can expect to live for six months, some will live longer than that, and some will live less than six months. Statistics allow us to give some ranges but never to make a prediction about how long an individual person will live. We can only hope for the best but need to prepare for the worst."

—Oncologist Lidia Schapira

Living (for Years) with Metastatic Disease

When Rita tells her teenage son and daughter that she doesn't feel that great, they'll go, "Oh, oh, oh, we're pulling the cancer card today!" And Mom will say, "Doesn't cancer count for anything?" Then they all burst out laughing.

Seven years ago, Rita was diagnosed with metastatic breast cancer—it had spread to her bones. She's gone through a lot of treatments: surgery, chemotherapy, radiation. She takes twenty pills a day and has a monthly injection. Sometimes the meds make her cranky and tired. Sometimes she cries. And she seems to catch every cold that comes her way. But she manages to keep working and be a mother to her two teenage children.

You may have a parent in Rita's situation: diagnosed with metastatic cancer but able to "manage" the cancer and live a fairly normal life. There are, of course, no guarantees with metastatic disease. A medicine might cease to be effective. Drugs might cause troubling side effects. Then again, a new medicine might come along and give the patient more time with fewer side effects.

"We've learned to make drugs that help switch off the signals inside cancer cells that lead to growth," says oncologist Lidia Schapira. "So we have been able to stop many of these cancers that in the past just grew and took over and killed. We've managed to keep them at bay."

Although she adds: "Cancer cells typically get smart and develop resistance. No intervention works indefinitely."

So there is no hope of cure for a patient with metastatic disease. Rather, there is life with cancer—a life that can continue for years if the patient is fortunate.

• •

Teens cope with a parent's metastatic disease in a variety of ways—pretty much the same ways teens cope with cancer in general. They grow closer to their parent. They're mad at their parent for having cancer. They take out their anger on the other parent. They're afraid of the uncertain future.

"Remember," says oncology counselor Shara Sosa, "whatever you're thinking about cancer, your parents are thinking it, too. Whatever you're afraid of, your parents are, too." Go ahead: be angry, cry, share your feelings.

And share the information about your parent with your

school. In the months and years ahead, it can be helpful if teachers know that "something is always present in this child's life," says Sosa. Teens might tell teachers and friends if they prefer a "no questions" policy or welcome periodic inquiries.

If you're lucky, friends can give you support. They can also give you grief. Lizzy, whose mother has metastatic cancer, had a so-called friend—we'll call her Monica—who would repeatedly say to other classmates: "You know Lizzy's mother is dealing with *a lot.*" And she'd say it in front of Lizzy.

Lizzy didn't like that one bit. She felt her "friend" was bullying her. So Lizzy formed an "I hate Monica" club. And you know how that goes. Monica found out and told her mom, who called Lizzy's mother and asked, "Why does your daughter hate my daughter?"

Perhaps Lizzy could have given her friend the benefit of the doubt, suggests social worker Sara Goldberger. Maybe she could have said: "I really appreciate that you care about my mom but you gotta stop this because it doesn't help me."

And these kind of uncomfortable moments can be balanced by life lessons. Watching her mom's determination to stay active despite the toll that cancer and its treatments take, Lizzy found inspiration for her college essay. Here's what she wrote: "You need to have a sense of humor. You can't put stuff off. And you can't take anything for granted."

• •

Conor's Story: Family Dinners Rule
Life is definitely different now for Conor of Maryland, a tenth-grader whose mom was diagnosed with metastatic breast cancer in 2006. For one thing, he's doing better in school than he used to.

"My mother always tells me her strongest wish is for me to do better. It's like I know if I do bad, she'll be really disappointed and she can't handle that right now." That does put some extra pressure on him, he admits. But he finds ways to deal—exercise, a couple of hours of video-game playing on weekends. "For those two or three hours," he says, "I'm just worried about the game."

Family togetherness is a priority. "We do a lot more stuff together, always eat together, don't take dinner upstairs." The family eats at the dining room table…and he and his parents actually Talk to Each Other.

Mom keeps Conor informed about her condition. "There are always ups and downs," he reports. "Life is as normal as it can be, I guess," he says.

His frame of mind: "You can never give up. There's always options out there."

12.4 Finding Hope When Things Seem Hopeless

Not every patient with a tough prognosis is fortunate enough to count on the cancer being "managed" for years to come. Your parent may have only a limited time ahead. How do you get through? How do you live day by day with this knowledge? Do you cry the whole time? Do you live in denial?

One thing that will help you get through the months ahead is open communication. If this book had a motto, it would be: speak the truth! That goes for parents as well as teens. If your parents aren't telling you the honest truth about what's going on, you'll end up frustrated and angry.

> "I didn't know for a long time that my mom wasn't getting better," says Stephanie, fourteen, of Utah. She now wonders, in retrospect, "Why didn't she tell me that?"

> Allison B. of Idaho, thirteen, whose dad died of prostate cancer, has the same complaint: "My mom and my dad, more

specifically my mom, kind of kept the severity of his cancer from me until like three months before he died. And so I was kind of mad about that. 'Cause I didn't know it was that bad."

"Honesty is the best policy," echoes Meghan of Ohio, fourteen. "My dad wasn't telling me what was happening. I had to weed it out. My parents would talk about it when they thought I wasn't around. I'd stay up and try to hear what was happening. It was the only way to find out. They were very protective; they didn't want me to get too worried." But their silence made her even more worried.

Some kids use the Internet to figure it all out. Child life specialist Kathleen McCue met with a fifteen-year-old girl who knew her dad was sick, who'd overheard her parents talking, and who suspected that his cancer was potentially fatal. No one in the family was talking to her about the details. She finally confessed to Kathleen, "I know my dad's probably going to die. I googled his cancer and it said almost everyone dies of it."

She knew that her parents thought they were being helpful by withholding the grim news. That wasn't helpful at all. Yet she, too, engaged in the same kind of protective behavior when it came to her two younger sisters, who were ten and twelve. Kathleen asked if she'd shared the news with them. Her response: "Oh no, I would never let them know about this."

Words of Wisdom:

One teenage boy's dad was the one who helped him cope with the dire prognosis. "He knew what it was. He knew it was going to kill him, and he was okay with that," the teen said. His dad's philosophy was: "Okay, if I'm going to die, I will die happy. I will die doing things with my family that I wanted to do." So Dad, who always helped his son deal with problems big and small, set an example that helped the son through the biggest tragedy of all.

So we all do it. We all try to keep things from each other. And that never works out well.

Then again, facing the truth isn't easy either. "I just didn't believe it was in the realm of possibility that she could die," says Jenny Fisher of her mom.

12.5 Living for the Moment

"Cancer is a wake-up call. It's like, oh, you've been putting this trip off for a couple years. So you should do it now because you don't know if you're going to be able to do it with the entire family."

—Liahona, fourteen, of Utah, whose
mother is battling breast cancer

So there you are: a teenager. With a parent who has cancer. And the prognosis is not good.

Words of Wisdom:

Living for the moment may be easier for you than for your parents. "I think kids are very good at being able to switch between realities," says Richard Ogden. "The reality of their mother dying and the reality of enjoying their life, loving their mother, looking forward to doing things. I think kids have a better capacity to immerse themselves in the moment. I don't want to generalize, but I think most kids can naturally do that."

"It wouldn't be a good idea to completely deny the fact and act as if everything is fine," says psychologist Richard Ogden, whose wife died of breast cancer when the couple's three children were ages six, twelve, and seventeen.

On the other hand, if all you do is focus on the loss, you won't be able to live in the moment. You want to "be with that person while he's still alive," Ogden stresses. You have to find your way to a middle ground where you don't deny the tragic facts but you also don't let them overwhelm you to the point where you can't spend time with the parent who's dying.

All those books about living for the moment, about the "power of now," may seem hokey or not something you'd be interested in. Until now.

> "Just be as full-hearted and loving and connected to one another as you can manage over this time. Savor and cherish your time. Don't spend it just feeling down in the dumps. You don't want to have false hope. Hope is an important thing to have."
>
> —Social worker Bunty Anderson

Marlene's Story: Sweet Sixteen in Dad's Hospital Room
Marlene had a sixteenth birthday party unlike any other. Her dad was in the hospital, recuperating from surgery related to his cancer. He wanted to surprise his daughter, so he got the nurses to decorate the room and ordered food he wasn't supposed to have. He and Marlene celebrated and watched pay-per-view movies: a horrible sequel to *Legally Blonde* and a shoot-'em-up Western were the only two available.

P.S. Part of living in the moment is living your own life, too. Marlene was torn: should she go on a church-sponsored mission to Mexico when her dad was facing surgery? Her dad told her, "I want you to go. I'll be here when you get back." And he was right about that.

Other kids have shared similar stories. They kept busy with school and friends. They went to sleep-away summer camp—with the understanding they might be called back home if the parent takes a turn for the worst.

12.6 A Different Kind of Hope

"You can hope your parents won't be in pain, that they won't be uncomfortable," says social worker Marisa Minor. "You can hope you'll be able to cope with the loss of that parent and hope your parent knows how much they're loved." (Hint: tell them!)

You can also hope for nice moments with your parent. "I mean, life is always both wonderful and tragic," says social worker Bunty Anderson. "We don't tend to pay much attention to the dark side, but we've all experienced it. Don't waste time on feeling horrible. It takes you nowhere and you never get that time back. Delight in the time you have with your parent."

Who knows, maybe you'll even get to go to Disney World.

12.7 What If You Feel Closer to the Parent with Cancer?

Cancer doesn't follow any rules. It may end up afflicting the parent you're closer to, the parent who really "gets" you. You may feel you're going to be left living with a parent who doesn't really know who you are or what makes you tick, who is distant, who is hard to talk to.

> "I'm kind of scared what will happen once my mom dies. What's my dad gonna do? He doesn't really understand."
> —Liahona, fourteen, of Utah, whose mom's cancer is not curable

One thing to remember: it's perfectly normal to be closer to one parent than the other. It doesn't mean you're an unloving child.

Even if you secretly (or not so secretly) wish that the other parent had cancer, the one you aren't as close with, that's normal, too.

Another thing to remember: relationships can change. A nineteen-year-old girl whose mom died of cancer, says: "I used to hate my dad a lot. Now he's my best friend. In a sad way, cancer brought us a lot closer." Maybe, she says, that's because even though you feel that cancer is tearing your family apart, "everyone is so angry at the same thing."

12.8 AVOIDANCE

You might find yourself unwilling or unable to spend a lot of time with your sick parent. "Sometimes you want to preserve the picture of the parent as they were at the top of their game. For that reason, some children may stay away. They love their parent so much they can't bear to see them sick and not all the way themselves," says psychiatrist Paula Rauch. "And those are two equally loving ways" to react to a parent who is suffering from cancer.

Then again, you might avoid your mom or dad because you're mad. Maybe harsh words were exchanged too many times.

Can you do anything about that?

You might be really upset inside. Maybe you thought someday you and your parent would work things out. Now the clock is ticking. When kids lose a parent, they'll sometimes say, "I always thought Mom or Dad would live long enough for us to get to be friends."

It's a huge burden for the teen to be the one to approach the parent and say, "I'm really sad that you have cancer…"

If you try to offer an olive branch, that might start a conversation that leads to good things. Or it could go nowhere, depending on your parent. Some people are capable of change. Some aren't. Maybe you need to enlist an ally—your other parent or another adult who can be a kind of moderator between you and your cancer-stricken parent. This is a case where a counselor, therapist, or support group can be immensely helpful.

"My dad and I had some differences. I tried to mend them. I did try to be close with him. Even though I never admitted it to myself, in the back of my head there was always the possibility that he might not make it."

—Mansoor of New Jersey, whose dad died
of cancer after a five-year struggle

12.9 Making Memories

Steven wanted to take pictures of his dad, who was diagnosed with lymphoma and then contracted serious infections after chemo. His dad didn't want to be photographed. He felt like he didn't look good because of the impact of his cancer treatments, and that's true. He was pale, thin, bald.

Dad's refusal to sit for a photo or video made Steven sad and angry. "I got so mad. My dad never liked to be in videos or pictures. I regret not just coming up to him and saying, 'Dad, five minutes.'"

Now, Steven says, "The only time I can hear his voice is on our answering machine for two seconds: "Hi, Heinz family, leave a message.'"

No matter how noble your intent, you can't force your parent to say "cheese." "I know that many people dying from cancer want to be remembered as who they were throughout their life, rather than having the focus be on the six to twelve months that they were sick with cancer and its treatment," says social worker Jill Taylor-Brown of CancerCare Manitoba.

But you can ask. The worst that will happen is that your parent will say, "No."

When the end is really near, when your parent is in the hospital or in hospice care and may have only hours or days left, you may be afraid to be with them. It might seem scary or depressing. And it can be both of those things.

Survival Tip: Sometimes, the solution is in the written or spoken word. Make up a list of questions you've always been curious about. Ask your mom or dad: what was your favorite thing to do on the playground when you were a kid? Did you get punished a lot when you were growing up? Why did you want to be a [fill in the parent's job]? Who did you take to prom? What's the worst (and best) thing that ever happened to you in school? What was the first thing you did when I was born? Write it all down. Or just casually ask, "Mind if I record this on my iPhone so I get it all?"

But like all things cancer, the matter of visiting at the end of life is complicated. As Rauch notes, "There's no redo."

Teens who found the strength to spend time with their parent in that difficult stage shared their stories with us. It was tough for them. But it meant a lot.

Reilly, sixteen, remembers when his seemingly invincible dad—a former Navy Seal—was in his final days, lying in a hospital bed and "really drugged." "I talked to him, I kept telling him I loved him. He opened his eyes and looked over. It was hard for him to talk. I would keep talking, being all gooey. I knew he was still around, I knew he heard me."

Words of Wisdom:
"We recognize that whether someone wants to see a family member in the very last days of their life, particularly if they're not able to talk, is not a litmus test of how much someone loves the parent. Some people feel that sitting at the bedside of someone who is confused and suffering is diluting the picture of the parent when the parent was himself."
—Psychiatrist Paula Rauch

. . . .

Marlene's Story: A Father, a Daughter, a Bratwurst

It looked as if Marlene Pierce's dad wasn't going to survive. Marlene tried to keep positive, but in the back of her mind she knew that her dad's death was a possibility.

Her dad was a typical dad in some ways. "He didn't sit and talk with us a lot," she recalls of his relationship with her and her younger sister. But when he knew he was pretty sick, he gave the girls a gift. "He sat us down and said, 'I don't know if I'm going to come out of this. I want to talk with you each one on one about anything or everything you want to ask me.'"

He didn't want any regrets. And Marlene remembers having this day with her dad, "and we just talked and talked. We were both crying and eating bratwurst, which he loved." And that, says Marlene, was the greatest gift her dad could have given her.

. . . .

Chapter 13

Losing a Parent to Cancer

This is a chapter we hope you don't have to read. It's about losing a parent to cancer.

We all go through a gamut of emotions, from grief to guilt, after someone we love dies. We cry, of course. Or sometimes we think we should cry and can't. And sometimes we laugh at a moment that's just crazy absurd, like the well-meaning friend who says, "I know how you feel—my gecko just died."

This chapter will talk about all of the emotions that may strike—and how to begin the process of healing.

13.1 A Dictionary of Emotions

So how do you feel? We asked a lot of teens who lost a parent to cancer. And we asked therapists who've worked with grieving teens to share their stories. Here's what they said:

Angry at the parent (and even at themselves): Hakeem's dad died of pancreatic cancer. Hakeem was angry at his dad for not taking better care of himself. When his dad first had stomach pains, he put off tests and treatment to finish an important work project. Hakeem wonders if perhaps the outcome might have been different if his dad had gone for treatment sooner.

Hakeem was also a bit angry at himself: could he have "pushed harder" for his father to go to the doctor? He now realizes that nothing he could have said would have changed his strong-willed father's mind.

Words of Wisdom:
"I had somebody in my support group today express that both his parents died from cancer, and he had feelings of relief that it was finally over. And I wanted him to know that that's very normal."

—Children's bereavement counselor Shavaun Jones

Full of regret: "I wish I would have been there more for my dad," says Erin, whose parents were divorced when her father was diagnosed with lung cancer. She lived in Florida, and her dad was in Ohio. She wishes she'd talked to him more on the phone, written him more letters, asked him what he needed and how he was feeling. "That's my regret—just not having been more there for him." Erin was seventeen when her father died.

Strange: "I felt like I was floating. I kid you not."

—Bianca of Virginia, seventeen, whose dad died of cancer five years ago

Blaming themselves: When his father died, Steven thought about karma: "If I didn't make this bad decision two weeks before, maybe he wouldn't have passed away." Even though Steven rationally knows that his bad decision wasn't the reason his dad died.

Bummed out: "It's like a slap in the face. Man, it sucks."

—Bianca

Relieved: "The moment he actually did pass away, there was a very peculiar feeling. It was extremely, extremely relieving. It's hard to find the right word without sounding weird about it, [but] it was very peaceful to know he wasn't in pain anymore."

—Mansoor, whose dad was diagnosed with cancer when Mansoor was around twelve and died five years later

Maybe even able to laugh: Dorrie, twelve, remembers

sitting with some classmates, eating lunch outside on a field trip, after her mom's death. "Someone I didn't know said, 'I hear there's someone in this group whose mom died.' No one seemed to think it was such a big deal. Then they find out it's me." In retrospect she says, "It was kind of hilarious."

Survival Tip: "You may miss your dad, but you may also think about how he was struggling to breathe and how hard it was. And you would love to have your healthy dad back but wouldn't want Dad to continue to be feeling the way he was feeling those last days."

—Psychiatrist Paula Rauch

Wishing that the *other* parent had died: "At a support group," says child life specialist Kathleen McCue, "a grieving teen will sometimes say, 'I'm so ashamed, I feel so bad, I wish it was my other parent who had cancer.' Then the kid will change the subject, maybe get up and walk around because just saying it has made him or her so uncomfortable."

If you have these thoughts, you may think: *what's wrong with me?* Nothing.

Words of Wisdom:

"Grief is inconvenient and it's not in your control. That's the hallmark of grief. It's going to bubble up. But if you let yourself feel your feelings, you can have some mastery of them. If you feel it *now*, it's not going to come up for the rest of your life. You have to feel your grief."

—Grief counselor Monica Coreman

"It's normal," says McCue. If one parent is easier to be with, if one parent gets you, and that is the parent who dies of cancer, it's normal to wish that the tables had been turned. And that doesn't mean you don't love the parent who survived.

13.2 MOURNING DOESN'T COME WITH AN EXPIRATION DATE

After a parent's death, you may find it is harder to get back on track that you thought it might be. Grief is a funny emotion. It can pop up months, years, after the death.

"Even when your parent dies," says Kaitlin, whose mom passed away two years after being diagnosed with cancer, "sometimes that's just the beginning."

• •

Sibling Story: Brother and Sister, Grieving Differently
"It was this huge explosion of grief when she died," says Tommy, fourteen, whose mom was diagnosed with oral cancer. She seemed to be doing okay as she went through treatment and then, in a startling turn of events, died two months later—a reaction to her treatment. After Tommy's big moment of grief, he says, "The grief subsided into the background. It lingered while I digested it. I'm slowly getting over it." He had a summer to get through. The family hadn't planned any activities for the kids because of the cancer fight. "The whole summer you just sit there and think about it," he says.

His sister, Dorrie, twelve, has a slightly different memory of him: "You spent the entire summer playing video games." About herself, she says: "I'm more long and drawn out. I worry more than he does."

• •

Survival Tip: *You Don't Always Have to Be Strong.*
"It's important to know that it's okay to cry, to talk about it, to vent and let your emotions out. I can't stand it when people tell someone to 'be strong' or 'stay strong.' That's absolutely the wrong advice. It's perfectly fine to be weak in times like these and

to seek help from friends, family, professionals, a priest, or whatever," says Emil, who lost his mother to cancer when he was thirteen.

"Holding that in or trying to stay strong is a terrible way to deal with these feelings. I tried doing that myself, just burying those feelings inside, and it was a mistake. The healing process and just dealing with things is unimaginably difficult, but trying to do it alone, or not dealing with it all, is impossible. You'll do more harm than good."

"After my dad passed away, I tried to be optimistic and I didn't wear my emotions on my sleeve. I continued being the happy person that I was before (at least on the outside), and my friend said that I was too happy. It hurt me because she had no idea what I was going through and how I was really feeling."

—Leann, twenty-two, whose dad died of cancer when she was sixteen

13.3 ALL KINDS OF QUESTIONS

You may have lots of questions about your parent's death. The biggest questions may have no answers: why did this happen to my parent? My friend's mom had breast cancer and she survived. Why did my mom or dad have to die?

"At my dad's rosary service, they read something he wrote when he was really sick. And he wrote, 'Why?' Not, 'Why me?' But 'why did this have to happen?' And so that's another question I have."

—Allison B., thirteen, of Idaho

Worst Thing Said to Me:

"At my mother's funeral, multiple people told me that every-thing happens for a reason. What reason was there for a thirty-four-year-old woman to die and leave her twelve-year-old and sixteen-year-old motherless? I still haven't figured that one out."

—The sixteen-year-old daughter whose mom died of cancer

Speaking of funerals...you might well wonder: what about it? It may be your first. Part of you may not want to go. Don't listen to that part. Go. You can speak about your parent if you wish. For some teens that's a very powerful moment. Or you can be silent. That's absolutely fine.

You may worry: what if I cry? Go ahead and cry. "People are expecting you to cry," says social worker Sara Goldberger.

Words of Wisdom:

"There is no wrong way to grieve other than not to grieve."

—Child life specialist Kathleen McCue

You may also feel at a loss for words as funeral-goers come up and express their sorrow and grief and sympa-thy. Adults don't always know what to say, either. Goldberger has a simple and perfect sug-gestion: "Say, 'Thank you.'"

13.4 Life Goes On

For starters, you may feel as if you can't imagine how your life will go on, how you'll do all the things you usually do (or gave up doing during your parent's sickness).

• •

A Support Group That Broke the Rules

Social worker Seth Berkowitz used to run a support group for teens coping with cancer. Some of the teens had a family member who was probably going to pass away. Some of the teens had already lost a parent or another family member to cancer.

The rule in support groups is that mixing people with different experience isn't a good idea. They're dealing with different realities. The kids with a parent who's still alive might stress out listening to kids who lost a parent and might think, "Oh my gosh, my parent's going to die, too!"

Only in this case, the group worked. Berkowitz thinks it worked because the kids with a parent still alive could see that the kids who'd lost a parent were doing okay. They realized, "Even if my parent dies, look, these kids are okay. They're still coming to support group and going to school; they have boyfriends and girlfriends."

The big lesson was: there's life after a parent's death.

• •

After her mother died, Kaitlin says, her friends were "awesome." Kaitlin is a natural-born pessimist. Her friends lifted her spirits. They told her, "Keep your head up. You deserve to have fun. Don't feel guilty about things you have no control over. Get through school to the best of your ability. Have fun. And we will always be there for you."

> "Having one parent instead of the two I grew up with was a big adjustment. I had to be more independent and take care of myself, so I learned a lot, and I got closer to my dad and sister as well."
>
> —Emil, whose mom died of cancer when he was thirteen

> "I don't worry about things I used to. I used to care about what people think of me. I got a B this semester and I didn't die."
>
> —Gia of Baltimore

"I was afraid people would treat me differently after my mom died," says Stephanie, fourteen, of Utah. That's actually a pretty normal reaction.

"Teens think people aren't supposed to die, this isn't supposed to be happening," says grief counselor Monica Coreman. "Some kids go as far as to say they don't want their teachers or friends to know."

But the death of a parent is impossible to hide. When the news gets out, the results can be encouraging. "A lot of my friends' moms have stepped up to offer support," says Stephanie. Dads can offer support, too.

> "After my dad died, my mom decided to form this thing called the 'Council of Dads.' It's just a bunch of family friends that are really close. I think there are maybe six people on it. I just talk to them and they give me really good advice that my dad would've."
>
> —Allison B., thirteen, of Idaho

13.5 Dealing with Your Emotions

One thing you have to do is process your parent's death. "Process" is a word that psychologists and social workers like to use. It simply means: "coming to terms with your emotions and finding a way to let out all the emotions you feel."

> "It's taken me a long time to get back on my feet after her death. It's been pretty terrible and really frustrating at points but you can keep going. I spent a good couple of years in a cloud of confusion and emotions I couldn't articulate and didn't understand. But I was lucky enough to find people who were willing to work with me through it.
>
> "Therapy has been amazing. I've found good friends who are able to handle the big emotions I have from it, and I'm

slowly weaning off of the bad coping mechanisms I started as a result of her illness. It's a lot of work, but it's worth it to feel happy, aware, and self-assured again."

—Maggie, who was thirteen when her mom was diagnosed with cancer. Her mother died four years later. Maggie is now twenty-eight.

Talking about your emotions in a support group or with a therapist is one way to process, of course. And maybe that means talking about all the parts of your parent's personality, including parts that you didn't like.

There are many kinds of relationships with a parent. In bereavement groups, everyone talks about how Mom was such a saint, how Dad was perfect in every way. "Come on!" says social worker Sara Goldberger. Dad might have been a bastard before cancer, and cancer might not have changed him for the better.

"Halfway through a teen week support group, you'll hear people say, 'I used to get so mad at him. He was so stubborn.'"

If you can talk honestly about the parent you've lost, "that's progress," Goldberger believes. If you can admit that your parent who passed away had flaws, then you won't be creating an ideal portrait of your parent and maybe feeling guilty for being a less than ideal child. "The reality is that we're all human; we all have flaws," she says.

What if your mom or dad was a tough parent to deal with? Dad didn't get you. Mom always wanted more from you. Or you just felt estranged from the parent. "When someone close to you dies, it's the death of the dream," says Goldberger. The dream that maybe you and your parent would improve your relationship. "But once the parent is gone, it's over." You're left with the relationship that you had, not the one you dreamed of having. But you can still love them and mourn them even as you recognize their flaws.

Or maybe you are just stuck on the bad memories. In bereavement groups that she leads, child life specialist Kathleen McCue asks the teens to talk about their good memories of the parent who passed. Sometimes, she says, "they can't find them." Or maybe they do remember some good things, but what they really remember "is the time your parent lied to you, kept something from you they should have shared, was in a bad mood and grounded you."

Her message to the kids is that it's okay to talk about it: "We have a hard time convincing them that it's okay to tell us about times when the parent wasn't nice to them, when they wished they had a different parent." And what can you say to that? McCue notes: "Sometimes forgiveness doesn't happen; sometimes there is no resolution."

• •

Not Ready to Talk...Yet

Child life specialist Kathleen McCue knew a girl who was fourteen when her dad died of cancer. Let's call her Angie. Angie's mom made her come talk to McCue to help cope with all the emotions inside. "She was forced to come," McCue remembers. "She was very sad. But she was like, 'I just can't talk about it. Life has been horrible. I just want to get back to my life.'"

McCue respected Angie's state of mind: "That's where she was and needed to be." So she talked to Angie's mom and said, "You don't need to do anything right now. Let her take time, give her a chance."

She told Angie: "I understand you know what you need. You know yourself best." Then she added: "Let me tell you, there may come a time when you need to talk about your dad." Angie was like, "Okay, fine, whatever."

Five years later, McCue got a phone call: "This is Angie. Do you remember me? You told me when I was ready to talk about my dad, I could call you again. I'm in college, and I'm ready. I need to talk about it."

Listening in on a Support Group

There may or may not be a bereavement group in your area. A hospice organization may offer such a group for kids who have lost a parent to any disease. And some cancer organizations run bereavement groups as well. Here's what happened at such a group run by Life with Cancer, a support organization based in Fairfax, Virginia.

Bianca sweeps into the chilly church basement and unleashes a stream-of-consciousness monologue. "You know what we're doing Tuesday, I'm not going to school, I'm going to be all weepy, we're going to Great Falls and spreading my dad's ashes, I have so much homework to do it's crap. I have 101 in math, I was failing last year, now 101, boom! I'm starving, I didn't eat lunch today, I almost beat a girl up, I'm not suspended yet. I can't wait to tell you my story."

And the monthly session of a bereavement group for teens is off and running. Social worker Jenny Eckert is on hand to "facilitate," as they say in social work talk. Bianca, who's almost eighteen, started coming four years ago when she got into trouble at school.

"A lot of your grief has been expressed with anger," Eckert observes.

"I'm better but this girl picked the wrong time to mess with me," Bianca says. "I pushed her up against a locker. I told her, 'I have five years of anger to take out on your face.'"

This coming Tuesday will be five years since Bianca's dad died of cancer.

Tonight there are three other attendees: Reilly, sixteen, whose dad died of a rare cancer in 2009; James who is mourning the loss of his younger brother to cancer; and first-timer Steven, whose dad was diagnosed with lymphoma on June 11, 2010 and passed away June 12, 2011.

"Are you having a tough year?" Eckert asks.

Steven says, "Yeah."

The ground rules of the group, Eckert explains, are: "You say what you want to. We try to get you to say something but you don't have to."

Bianca says, "That's a lie. You try to make us say something!"

To break the ice, Eckert introduces an art project. The aim is to color in a shield and write the words on it that helped protect you after your parent's death.

Reilly says what helps him is "my attitude."

"Which attitude, your good one or your bad one?" Eckert asks.

Reillly admits: "I have a really short fuse. I throw chairs at teachers." He pauses. "I don't actually do that. But I'm really headstrong."

Eckert says, "But you have taken that attitude and done positive things with it."

Reilly says that he's involved in becoming a counselor-in-training at a camp for kids who've had a parent with cancer. "I'm really passionate about Camp Kesem," he adds.

Bianca has her passions as well. She has done two walk-a-thons to raise money for cancer, each about twenty miles. "I felt like crap, but it was good, it was positive, I was very proud." She adds: "I carried my dad's picture all twenty-one miles."

Eckert draws Steven into the conversation. He says, "I would just like to have every day be kind of better."

Bianca consoles him: "Slowly but surely things do get better. Don't get me wrong. I have my days when it feels like it's just awful."

They talk some more, sometimes about their parent who died, sometimes about how classmates annoy them, sometimes about random stuff. (Reilly makes fun of Bianca's jacket.) Then Eckert asks Steven if he wants to share his story.

After Steven's dad was diagnosed, Steven told him: "Dad, I can't handle losing you." His dad would smile and say, "I'm not gonna die." But chemotherapy weakened his immune system. He developed a stomach infection, and doctors said "there was no way he was going to beat that," Steven told the group.

When his dad did die, Steven remembers how lost he felt. "I, like, didn't know how to handle it. I couldn't cry. I just felt empty. I always play basketball. I would hold the basketball in my hand but I never even shot." His father was a pilot and he always left for trips. "I felt like he was away on a trip and was going to come home," Steven says.

Then Steven shares a moment of comfort.

"I knew my father made it to heaven," Steven said. "I prayed that night he died. I said, 'Can you give me a sign my dad has made it to heaven?' It's June 12, so not July 4 yet. I'm going to sleep. Right when I closed my eyes, I opened them again and there were fireworks outside the window. I took that as a sign my father made it to heaven and he's safe."

Now he has questions: "I don't know why the cancer was so aggressive. They said it was so random. I think after my father died, I thought about things more. I take every day as if it could be my last."

"Yes," Reilly agrees. "You gotta live life to the fullest."

"Within certain guidelines," cautions Jenny Eckert. Reilly gives the impression he doesn't always obey "guidelines."

"I kick people in the face," Reilly says with a grin. Actually that's part of his martial arts training. "Martial arts is a huge confidence builder," he says. A way of learning to cope with a loss that is simply unfathomable.

The conversations that December night show that another great way to cope is the chance to sit in a church basement for an hour, sharing memories and insights with other teens who've lost a parent to cancer.

13.6 School Can Be a Comfort...or a Pain

Maybe you'll be able to get back in the groove at school. Maybe it'll be a relief.

Or maybe not. You might do fine for a couple of weeks, and then something might trigger a memory of your parent. And you might not be able to concentrate. Or you might put your head down on your desk. Or act out and say something harsh to a classmate or the teacher.

That kind of unexpected grief is perfectly natural.

"Children and adolescents tend to grieve in spurts," says social worker Seth Berkowitz. "Today was a good day, fairly normal. Tomorrow is a bad day." Maybe it was a special day in your family and you miss your parent. Maybe it's the start of baseball season and you used to go to games with your dad.

Only now it hits you: "I'll never be able to do that again." So you come to school the next day with a bad attitude.

"Parents and educators need to recognize that kids are allowed to have a bad day even two or three years later."

Teachers may be very good teachers, Berkowitz says, but they may not get just how teenage grief works. "Teachers deal with the norm. Cancer is outside the norm." So if you've been coming to class and being a good student, and then on one particular day you act out, the teacher has no clue why— or that it is two years to the day since your mom or dad passed away.

This may be a time when you want to get your parent involved, helping you explain to a teacher or counselor why you feel the way you do. Because even great educators may not be so great in dealing with a child who's lost a mom or dad.

Problem: Steven's dad died in June, and that next year in school, Steven was struggling. His grades slipped, he sometimes fell asleep in class, and he sometimes trash talked to his classmates. Once he ripped up an assignment paper. Steven got sent to the vice principal, who, says Steven, delivered this message: "You can't be acting that way." Steven said, "I'm still trying to process everything."

The vice principal, says Steven, answered, "That only lasts for so long." And Steven said, "I know academics are important but that's not 100 percent of me. Right now I've got my own crap going on at home." And the principal was like, "You don't want to be here. I'm trying to teach you a lesson."

Possible Solution: Social worker Seth Berkowitz suggests that, with the help of your parent, and maybe your guidance counselor, you might ask that the vice principal and teachers be told that "You shouldn't be saying 'Get over it.'" "Grief is not a five-day or two-month process," says Berkowitz. "It's not even that in the adult world. It's a multi-year process."

What if the school says to the parent, "Why, no one on our staff ever said such a thing"? Then the parent might be a diplomat, says child life specialist Kathleen McCue. Instead of getting into the "who said what" argument (which isn't likely to help anyone), the parent might say, "I'm glad you understand how difficult teenage grief is."

13.7 Music Can Make It Better

Music may have helped you cope during your parent's illness. And it may help you cope if you lose your parent.

Jackie took a singing lesson after her dad died. She was fine all day in school, she recalls. Then she walked into the lesson and just started bawling. The teacher had no idea what to do. "We just talked," she says, "and that really helped."

Before he died, she was working on a song that her dad had wanted her to sing, a nostalgic song called "American Lullaby." She wasn't quite ready to sing it for her dad. When he was in good health, she'd tease him, "You'll hear me on your deathbed."

"It was a total joke," Jackie says.

But she did sing it to him before he died. The song is now a way to keep her dad in her mind. She also finds comfort in listening to the song "If I Die Young" by the Band Perry, in which the narrator, who does indeed die too young, tries to comfort those left behind.

Kelly, twelve, whose dad died a year ago, is also a fan of "If I Die Young." "It's like my dad's favorite song," she says. "I feel connected to Dad when I hear it."

13.8 STAYING CONNECTED

Your parent is gone, but you still want to feel close. You're worried—will I have to look at a picture to remember what Dad's eyes looked like?

> "Sometimes I can't remember what my dad sounded like. I called his cell phone every day for two months to listen to his voice. And I see his face on a video and just expect him to walk through the door."
>
> —Reilly, sixteen, of Virginia

Here are some of the simple rituals and keepsakes that grief counselor Monica Coreman has proposed.

If you like one of the ideas, she says, just do it. That'll give you a little bit of a feeling that you're in control, as well as a way to keep the memory of your parent close to your heart.

- **Make a scrapbook.** It can be digital or paper. Memories do fade. A scrapbook is a way to preserve them.
- **Carry a picture.** "Teenagers don't always want to put their grief out there for everybody else," says Coreman. "I'm big on giving them private ways to grieve." One teenager was sad that her dad couldn't be at her high school graduation. Coreman suggested pinning a small picture of her dad to the inside of her gown. Having her dad's image with her made her feel that, in a way, he was there with her.

  While this kind of commemorative ritual sounds like it would appeal more to girls than to boys (sorry for sexual stereotyping), Coreman says, "I've had boys do stuff like that." She'll ask a teenage boy about an upcoming milestone: "Do you need your dad there?" The boy might say, "Yes." She'll say, "Put a picture in your pocket." Or keep one on your cell phone.

- **Wear something that belonged to the parent.** Wear a watch, put a ring on a chain around your neck. One girl kept and wore her mother's socks. Some kids want to hang on to a favorite T-shirt or jacket, which may carry the faint hint of a parent's aroma.
- **Carry a stone.** Coreman might give a glass stone to a teenager and tell him or her to talk about memories when holding the stone. The teen can keep the stone in a pocket and keep those memories close as well.
- **Light a candle.** In Jewish tradition, a memorial candle is lit on the anniversary of a family member's passing away. The flame flickers and in a mysterious way you feel closer to the person who's gone. In a similar vein, Coreman suggests that teenagers might consider candle therapy.

"One thing we've done is light a candle on all the holidays or special days" as a reminder of the parent, she said. In some households, she adds, family members will share memories on such special occasions as well. In others, "if you have bitter adults, you're not allowed to do that." She recalls a teenage girl whose mom wouldn't let anyone talk about the dad. The teen decorated a candle and lights it on her birthday and other special occasions—a way of staying connected to her dad.

You can also remember a parent without any tangible objects.

"There's not a day that I don't think about him. Every time I play tennis, snow ski, water ski...those are things he taught me to do. Every time we go on a hike, I think how great it would be to have him here."

—Morgan of Seattle, whose dad was diagnosed with cancer when she was fifteen and died a year later

"If your parent passes away, don't pretend they don't exist. Keep their memory with you. It can really help you. If you have a hard time, think about what they would have told you to do."

—Stephanie, fourteen, of Utah

. . . .

Reflections from Jenny

When Jenny Fisher was seventeen, she lost her mom to cancer. Here are her memories:

The night before she died: "It became clear to me that she was going to die. I remember I cried very hard. My dad just let me cry. My sister kind of freaked out because I was crying hysterically."

How nature helped: "My family took me on a trip. We went to the ocean, just to get outside. February is pretty cold to be going to the ocean. I walked on the beach. That really helped."

How a friend helped: "A friend called me and I told her. She told my teachers. It really helped that I didn't have to do it myself."

Why she didn't like telling people: "Now I'm going to be the poor girl whose mom died."

What she liked to hear from friends: "I know you're sad, and I'm sad that you're sad."

How she's changed from the experience: "I try to make sure I spend time with my family members. Even though I live far away, I call come home regularly, call my grandparents, see the people I love."

A good thing and a bad thing about her boyfriend: "He is very supportive. He is a great listener. But sometimes he says things like, 'My mom tried to make this dish I liked and she totally failed.' I try not to say, 'You're lucky you have a mom.'"

Precious memories: "My mom really liked *Gone with the Wind*. We watched it together. We shared books. I would just come talk to her after school about the little things, tell her how my day went."

How her mom's cancer changed her: "If she hadn't been sick, I probably would have rebelled in some teenage way."

• •

• •
Bianca: Five Years Later

Bianca had two huge adjustments to deal with at once. Her dad died of cancer when she was twelve, and then weeks later the family moved to another state. She has a lot of advice to share:

Note: Therapists say that if a parent was cremated, some teens don't like the idea of spreading all of their parent's ashes. They often want to hold on to some of the ashes as a tangible symbol of their parent.

The questions: "People are scared to ask you: how did it happen? Why did your dad die? When I first moved here, I couldn't get the words out, now it's easier to talk. I hate when people creep around and are afraid to ask about my father. I love to talk about my dad."

Dad's legacy: "He told me before he died that life is too short to hold a grudge against someone. We don't need to be mad all the time."

The ashes: "We're going on a hike and will spread some of his ashes. I was freaking out, saying, 'I don't want to spread all of his ashes.' My mom was like, 'We're not. Calm down.'"

• •

• •

Cait's Story: A Burden and a Blessing

Cait is twenty-one, slim, with dark, flashing eyes. She lost her mom to cancer a couple of years ago. Cait was the middle child—she has an older sister and a younger sister. The three sisters all cared about their mom deeply. But during the five years that their mother fought the disease, they reacted in different ways.

"Their way of dealing was scheduling things so they couldn't be home," says Cait. "Oh, I have play rehearsal, I'm blah-blah-blah, some bull*** excuse not to be in the house. It's not like they were useless. They were just more impatient and unreliable with caring for my mom."

Cait was the one who stayed at home. "I was with my mom the most. I helped her with basic bodily functions. I tried to make sure she had as much privacy as possible." And she quit her high school soccer team because of the demands on her time. "That was really hard for me, but we all made sacrifices."

Cait's mom had brain cancer. Sometimes the cancer would make strange words flow out of her mother's mouth. She cursed a lot. But sometimes her mother was extremely clear in what she said. Once she told Cait, "You are the only one who cares about my feelings."

Yet even words of praise didn't make it easier to be her mother's primary caregiver. "It sucked at times, like most of the time," she says. "But when we got a good moment, a moment that reminded me of how my mother used to be, my sisters weren't there for that and I was. I paid a price but it was worth it."

Her father knew how much he leaned on Cait. One day he told her, "I can't do this without you. I can't depend on your sisters, and I can't do it on my own. You will have to be there with me. I don't know how long it's going to last."

Cait doesn't romanticize the experience. "It wasn't picture perfect," she recalls of her caregiving for her mom. "I dealt with the stuff no one else wanted to deal with."

Cait realized that she wouldn't be able to fully lead her own life until "someone comes out of nowhere and saves me" (highly unlikely) or "my mom dies."

Yet she didn't want her mom to die. So she realized, "You can't win."

She couldn't win with her sisters, either. As Cait remembers it, "They didn't want to deal with the responsibility." When the three girls were all home, that didn't work out so well. "We'd rip each other's heads off. You'd think we would want to work together, but we just took our frustrations out on each other."

And then came the time when Cait's mom was truly dying. "Everyone was scrambling to be with her," Cait remembers. "I was with her for five years. And I can live with myself."

In a funny way, the whole experience actually ended up bringing the girls closer together. "You share some things no friend could ever share with you," Cait's mom used to tell her daughters. Now when the three of them remember their mother, Cait says, the memories "keep us from ripping each other's heads off, even help us to act like a family again."

• •

• •

Ryan's Good-Bye

Ryan Urich has vivid memories of the last days of his father, actor Robert Urich.

"Halfway out the door from visiting my father in the

hospital, I remember thinking, Maybe I should go back and say good-bye again, like just in case.

"My mom's like, 'No, you'll see him later.'

"So I was like, 'Okay.'"

And then Ryan got the call that his dad was really dying. "I freaked out. I tried to get it together to go back. Should I bring my ukulele? I didn't know what to do or think.

"I was going over 100 mph to the hospital. I'm honking and blinking my lights and hauling ass.

"The officer pulled me over. He said, 'You were going over 100 mph.'

"I said, 'My father is in the hospital. They're intubating him.'" [That's inserting a breathing tube.]

The cop wrote a ticket but didn't impound the car.

"I saw my dad on the ventilator. We had a vigil. It felt like a week, but it was maybe two days. Everyone kind of lined up to give him a hug, whisper something in his ear.

"We'd hear one breath, wait thirty seconds, think, 'That's it,' and then there'd be another breath."

And then, he was gone.

"The next morning we went out to breakfast. Then we went home. I took my little sister to her room and lay down in the bed next to her. I heard the door slam, thought I heard his father's voice, almost felt a presence in the room. I shut my eyes. I was so afraid to open my eyes, that I might see him. And eventually, I did open my eyes. And my father wasn't there.

"That was kind of when I realized…"

At this point, telling this story nearly ten years after the fact, Ryan begins sobbing. "Just a second," he says. Then he finishes the story:

"That was when I realized that I would never see him again."

• •

Vern's Loss—and His Gift

It's especially hard to lose a parent as a teenager. But it's hard at any age. Vern Yip, a designer who's starred on several shows on TLC and HGTV, including *Deserving Design*, lost his mom to cancer when he was thirty-six. That was in 2006. He still misses her.

"She was my best friend, my inspiration," he says. Her last days were painful, both for her and her son. "One night it was so bad that she looked at me and said, 'Please, please help me die.' It was the absolute low point for me. I just kept telling her, 'It's okay, whenever you want to go you should just go.'"

From the despair of his loss, Yip has built something positive. He and his sister established the Vera Yip Memorial College Scholarship Fund through the Ulman Cancer Fund's National College Scholarship Program. The scholarship is open, he says, to "all these kids who had cancer, or had a very close family member who had it, who are still trying to pursue an education despite all the challenges in their life."

Vera Yip's belief in the value of education was a motivating factor. "She used to say, 'Never stop learning. They can take away your money, your house, all your possessions, but they can't take away your education.'" She was one of fifteen children in her Chinese family, he says, and was the most educated by far: "She always believed in being a trailblazer."

In her memory, Yip is helping teens and young adults affected by cancer to blaze their own trails.

Chapter 14

The New Normal: Life After Cancer

Welcome to the "new normal."

"New normal" is part of the vocabulary you'll hear in the cancer world. Survivors use it, oncologists use it, therapists use it. You might end up using it, too.

Q: What is the "new normal"?

A: While your mom or dad is being treated for cancer, you're in a temporary state, a kind of limbo, where everything is at least a little bit different due to the presence of the illness in your family. When cancer is out of your family's life, things are supposed to go back to normal. But life will never be exactly the same as it was before cancer. This is the "new normal."

Because cancer is complicated, there are several kinds of "new normals." In some cases, your parent passes away. That is a new normal tinged with deep sorrow (see Chapter 13). Then there are families where the parent continues in a kind of limbo with metastatic disease that requires ongoing

Words of Wisdom:

"I truly believe that [a parent's cancer] is a real opportunity to teach so many important lessons and skills for life. Such as empathy, such as open and honest communication, such as showing how families can come together in a crisis and work as a team and be stronger for it. Teenagers will say they wish it didn't happen, but having had the experience is a big part of what made them who they are."

—Social worker Barbara Golby

treatment. So a lot of the emotions that cancer brought up may stay with you and your family.

And then there's the new normal that begins when your parent has finished active treatment and is doing okay.

You may think: great! I can finally get my life back on track, and our family will go back to the way we were before cancer. In reality, life might not be the same as before. Cancer is a major experience that will probably have a permanent impact on your family. Think about it this way: wouldn't it be weird if *nothing* changed?

> "When bad stuff happens now, you realize it's nowhere near as bad as what happened with my dad. It helps you cope with whatever happens. You think, 'Oh well, things could definitely be a lot worse.' I remember when my dad woke up every night sick, coughing up a lung. It puts everything in perspective."
>
> —Tyler R. of Virginia. His dad was treated for lymphoma when Tyler was in middle school. Dad is now doing fine and Tyler is in high school.

Some new normal changes may include (but are not limited to):

1. New appreciation for parents and life.
2. More empathy for others.
3. No patience for friends who fret about trivial things.
4. Fears: Will the cancer come back? Will I get cancer, too?
5. Different ideas about what you want to do with your life.

Maybe the experience of watching a parent battle cancer will change you dramatically. Then again, you may just want to resume the life you had and never think about cancer again. Or maybe you fit somewhere in the middle—changed a bit but happy to be back in a household where cancer isn't running the show.

Your parents will definitely play a role in defining this new normal. "What happens sometimes," says child life specialist Kathleen McCue, "is that parents have changed and aren't going to change back. They use time differently; they're more strict, less strict; they feed the family different food. That throws the teen off."

Yet a lot of the new normal choices—about what's important to you, about how you spend *your* energy—are up to you. It's kind of like a video game where you can pick the level you want to play. And you don't have to play at the same level as your siblings or your parents.

14.1 WHAT HAPPENS NOW?

Going through a parent's cancer exposes you to the fact that there are bigger problems out there than a gossiping friend or a killer math test.

> "My mom never got angry at anyone for asking intrusive questions. She took it that the reason they were asking was a positive thing and that people cared. She was just calm and so even keeled about everything. She was pretty amazing, I hope if I'm ever faced with anything similar that I can face it and face everyone else just as gracefully as she did and as confidently and as strongly as she did."
>
> —Alison S. of Washington State. Her mom was treated for breast cancer when Alison was fourteen and is now in good health.

> "It did change me. It kind of taught me you only have twenty-four hours in a day, and once they're gone, you don't get them back. Live every day like it's your last! But don't have regrets over what you could have done [differently]."
>
> —Jaclyn of Louisiana

14.1.1 Tightened Family Ties

Head Count: We asked our poll takers if cancer brought their family closer together or created conflict:

- 74% said it brought them closer together
- 26% said it created conflict

"I think it brought my mom and me a lot closer. We're buddies, great friends. Cancer makes you realize that you definitely don't know what you have until it's gone, or it's almost gone."

—Alex of Manitoba, whose mom is a breast cancer survivor

"I guess it sort of made me and my mom a lot closer and me a little bit less spoiled because before that I was a brat to everyone."

—Allison B., thirteen, of Idaho

"It changed my relationship with my mom. We don't focus on little things we used to fight about. Like doing the dishes. If she would ask me, normally I would have started an argument. And now, I just do the dishes."

—Miriam, a college student whose mother is a breast cancer survivor

Perhaps in your new normal, conversation might flow a bit more easily. Megan Boyer, thirteen, says of mother-daughter chats, post-cancer: "We've learned to talk to each other about everything."

And if you all have been honest with each other during the cancer experience, that honesty could set a new pattern for family communication.

"My children have told me over the years that the number-one thing that helped them most was that I was always honest," remembers Wendy Harpham, mother of three, who has been treated seven times for lymphoma. "This issue of trust has become a huge centerpiece for our lives. Whatever the challenge—even something insignificant like we're meeting for lunch and somebody's running late—we tell the truth. We tell the truth about where we are: are you just leaving, or are you really two blocks away? And we tell the truth about critical things, like when they ask, 'Mom, are you worried that your cancer will come back?'"

But what about the teens who don't feel closer to their parent(s) post-cancer? Sometimes, after a family goes through a hard time, the family members do "become more separate," says psychiatrist Paula Rauch. That doesn't make you an ungrateful or unloving child. That's just how it played out in your family.

And not everything needs to change. Your counselor or therapist and everyone who helped you through the cancer issues can still provide support and a sense of continuity.

14.1.2 PARENTS, STEP ASIDE: A NEW AND IMPROVED YOU

When your parent has cancer, you might develop new attitudes and skills in response. Maybe you're a better student. Maybe you've become a better driver (from shuttling around your younger siblings), a better cook (from helping out in the kitchen), or a supreme toilet cleaner.

> "My mom was always tired or in bed sleeping because of therapy. I did a lot more cleaning, laundry, cooking. I became pretty independent, and that's a good thing. When my mom got better, she realized, 'You kids really matured through this.' She liked it."
>
> —Alex of Winnipeg

Warning: Not every parent is ready for an Independent Teen. "Teens who have been helpful during their parent's cancer have taken on new responsibilities and kind of stretched to be more independent," explains child life specialist Kathleen McCue. "They want to continue that freedom and independence. And the parent wants you to be that kid again, to take back the parenting role." Plus, time has passed. You are six months, a year, two years older. Your parent may want to go back to parenting you *the way you were.*

So you and your parent may have a disagreement about, let's say, curfews.

There may be a blow-up.

Now what?

In the best of all possible worlds, says McCue, you and your parents will sit down and talk.

The communication skills you may have developed during the cancer period will no doubt come in handy during future parent-child negotiating sessions!

You have to realize that your parents are still your parents, so yes, there will be curfews and parental statements like, "I can't believe how much time you spend playing video games."

14.1.3 KEEPING UP THE SYMPATHY

As your parent's treatments wind down and their health improves, you may think: oh, cool, now I can be mean to Mom and Dad again without feeling bad and resume my lazy ways around the house. Sayonara, dishwasher and vacuum cleaner!

Not so fast! Even as your family moves forward, your parent who had cancer may still suffer lingering effects, both psychological and physical.

You, on the other hand, may not want to dwell on it. Family members tend to want to forget about the cancer much more quickly than the cancer survivor. The end of treatment may be the time when the survivor really thinks about what just happened. Plus, there may be lingering side effects from the treatments.

"When I really see people struggle the most is when treatment is over," says oncology counselor Shara Sosa. Sometimes you'll find yourself struggling. Or sometimes your parents will struggle and you simply won't have the patience to deal with it.

Survival Tip: Ask your parents how they're doing, and you might get an answer that explains a lot about how Mom or Dad seem to be behaving. Perhaps that answer might be: "I'm okay, the doctor says I'm doing great but it's going to take me a while to get back on my feet. It's nothing to worry about. I'll let you know if there's something to worry about. But you need to know all this chemotherapy has left me pretty tired and that's going to be in my system for a while."

Having another cancer-themed family meeting might be in order to talk about such issues. Elissa Bantug recalls a lack of "clear expectations of what was going to happen long term" after her mother finished treatment. She says there was "no conversation about survivorship and what that meant." All she knew was that "Mom wasn't going to jump back up and run around with us after treatment. She wasn't feeling well for a long time."

The other part of the "new normal" is keeping the experience as a part of your family. Remember the lessons learned. Maintain any improvements to your family dynamics—more family dinners, less fighting.

14.1.4 We're Survivors, Too!

Your parent is a survivor. What about you? There's a big debate in the cancer community about whether the word "survivor" can include family members.

Some family members think: no. They reserve the title of survivor for the person who battled cancer. Other family members think they deserve the title. And that's perfectly okay. The National Coalition for Cancer Survivorship defines survivor as not only the person diagnosed but also family members.

Words of Wisdom:

"You live with the fact that [your parent had cancer]. You try to find meaning, to see that, yes, you witnessed this and survived it. It gives you some appreciation for life, a knowledge that other people your age don't have, and that knowledge may allow you to understand things in future that other people don't."

—Psychologist Barry J. Jacobs

Some teens definitely agree with the expanded definition. And they want to be recognized as survivors.

That was an important topic in a focus group of fifteen- to eighteen-year-old African Americans run by Drexel University Professor Maureen Davey.

One girl said: "I don't really think we get recognition. I think they get recognition for being survivors (which they should), but we really don't because we are behind the scenes. But we really do a lot."

"Yeah, even though they are survivors, we are survivors, too," another teen said. "What they go through, we go through."

14.2 New Normal Hiccups and Surprises

No, you should not expect chronic cases of hiccups in the new normal. But there will be changes. Some of them will be positive: a new identity as a survivor, stronger family ties, a better version of you. But you also may see changes that are puzzling and frustrating.

14.2.1 Impatient with Your Friends

A major life experience like cancer can make you grow up a little faster, become more mature and a little wise beyond your years or the level of your peers (which may lead you to feel like saying *"Grow up!"* to your less mature friends).

Here are some of the comments we heard from teens at Camp Kesem, the camp for kids who have a parent with cancer:

Lance: "I feel like it helped me grow up a lot more. You take everything more seriously." [He pauses to wipe a tear from his eye.]

Abby: "You get a little more mature."

Lyndsey: "When I see lazy people, I get really mad. When people complain and won't do anything to fix it, that's my biggest pet peeve."

Just remember that you're in a different place than your friends. "I hear this from kids all the time," says child life specialist Kathleen McCue. "Comments like, 'My friends worry about such dumb things. I've learned what's really important to worry about.'"

Her advice: "Try not to personalize it." If you tell your friends, "I can't believe you're upset because the Nike store sold out of the shoes you want," then odds are, your friends will soon no longer be your friends. If you tell your friends, "you're obsessing about dumb stuff," they might pull away from you. Is that what you want to happen?

Instead, Kathleen McCue suggests you share your new outlook. You might say, "Since we had cancer in the family, things that used to be important to me aren't that important anymore." Or "It's just hard for me to hear you talk about things like that." You'll be letting them know where you now are.

And you may have made some new friends who were really there for you—and will continue to be there for you. "I gained many, many friends," says Megan.

Maya says: You kind of have to come to terms with the fact that suffering is suffering. Objectively, your friend's fight with her boyfriend or your buddy's lament over his upcoming physics exams might seem petty, but everyone's entitled to their feelings, even if the cause of the problem seems trivial. As a good friend, you can acknowledge this and be there for your friends, regardless of how silly or small their problems may seem. When you catch yourself judging your friend as they're complaining, remind yourself of this.

14.2.2 HEALTH CONSCIOUS AND OTHER LIFESTYLE CHANGES

Have you been eyeing your parent's grocery bags with suspicion? *What's up with the brussels sprouts, Mom?*

Post-cancer, your family may make some changes to their diet, to the products they buy, to their level of physical activity, to their medical check-up schedule, or to other parts of their lifestyle. Cancer—or any illness—can make you more aware of and conscientious about your health.

Watching your parent battle illness may also motivate you to become healthier. "I'm more aware of my own health than I used to be," says Alison S., now twenty-three, whose mom is a breast cancer survivor. "I graduated from college, I'm living on my own, have my own health insurance. I don't have my parents to tell me to get a checkup or remind me to do self-exams. After my mom went through that, it's just a given: I need to be aware of what's going on in my body."

Bailee, whose mom is also a breast cancer survivor, agrees: "We eat so much healthier. My sisters and I are more aware of what's going on with our bodies."

THE NEW NORMAL: LIFE AFTER CANCER

14.2.3 FEAR OF CANCER

Remember when we talked about how the word "cancer" may become charged with negative power after it personally affects you? How hearing it may send shivers down your spine? After your parent recovers from cancer, this fear of both the word and the illness may stick with you.

You may fear that the cancer could return. But that doesn't mean you need to live in fear.

The odds of a recurrence have a lot to do with the type of cancer and the stage of cancer. "And the longer you stay in remission, the more likely you are to stay in remission," says oncologist Anna Franklin.

You might also begin to worry that you will get cancer. Your mom or dad had cancer, so does that mean you're going to get it, too? Chapter 2 talks about the genetic component in cancer. At this time, most cancers are not considered to be influenced by your DNA.

Maybe you won't be scared. Maybe you'll be inspired by your parent's example. "I got lucky. Both of my parents are okay," says Alison S., whose mom had breast cancer and whose dad had bladder cancer. "If one of them had died, I would have a completely different story. But cancer doesn't scare me. I hope if it ever happens to me that I can deal with it with the same humor and positive outlook that my mom did."

Maya (and her sister, Daniela) say: It's easy to coax yourself into complacency: *whew! Cancer's gone, don't have to worry about it*...and not think about it for a while—outta sight, outta mind. Then from time to time, seemingly out of the blue, I'll get a fleeting anxiety about Mom's breast cancer coming back. And I'm always concerned about my own cancer risk. I manage that concern through health-consciousness for sure, trying to eat healthy, exercise, buy organic.

14.3 Struggling in the Aftermath

The experience of your parent's cancer may leave you with lingering negativity, perhaps in the form of anger and depression. Sometimes it's impossible to tease out—are your problems linked to your parent's cancer or would they have happened anyway?

> "Life is pretty normal currently regarding [my dad's] cancer," says a fifteen-year-old girl whose father has been fighting cancer for a year. "But I was recently diagnosed with an eating disorder and I'm currently still in treatment, so I'm not exactly sure what normal for my life is supposed to look like or feel like. As all of this is stressful, it just adds to the worries in our family."

Continuing to grapple with the experience of cancer in the family is normal, in fact, it's to be expected. Refer to the advice in Chapters 6 and 11 on coping and seeking support, which still holds true in the new normal.

14.4 Becoming an Activist

You may feel inspired or motivated (or like it's your duty) to help others whose lives are touched by cancer. Activism related to cancer can take a number of different forms—from raising money for families with cancer to talking openly about your experience, to volunteering for a cancer organization.

On the road to becoming Miss Black Louisiana USA, Jaclyn Brown took part in a lot of pageants. "My platform has always been breast cancer

Words of Wisdom:
Does one person's activism make a difference? Oncologist Mary Hardy says that it takes lots and lots of drops of water to make an ocean—and lots and lots of individual activists to make a difference in the war against cancer.

awareness. Even though I am only eighteen, I feel no matter how old you are, you should know that cancer can happen to anybody. It doesn't have a gender or age; it doesn't affect only blondes or brunettes. If you're human, you can get breast cancer. Even boys can get it."

• •

Making Lemonade from Lemons

Becoming a cancer activist—speaking out, volunteering, raising money for the cause—is a great way to make something positive out of a terrible experience (cancer).

Sonia Kashuk, a breast cancer survivor, nationally acclaimed makeup artist, and mother of two, raised money for cancer and inspired her daughter to do the same: "Cancer is no longer a death threat today. But it isn't a pretty word no matter what. You can't put a flower on cancer. I try to be an advocate for breast cancer and to help anybody that I can help. I try to raise awareness for the Breast Cancer Research Foundation (BCRF).

"I have my [makeup] products at Target stores to raise money. So my children see me taking something that happened to me and using it personally. A few years ago, my daughter Sadye was doing some kind of lemonade stand on the street. She took the money, the $50, and sent it to BCRF. I think seeing what I'm doing helps them see what they can do."

> "My dad had brain cancer. It was his idea to have a lemon-ade stand. My dad and a neighbor built it. We made fresh-squeezed lemonade, did it for four summers. We raised a thousand dollars for brain injury services and were on the national news. So many people showed up, it was so cool!"
>
> —Abby, fourteen, of Maryland

Sisters Gavi, sixteen, and Mia, thirteen, founded a cancer club at school after their mother's battle with breast cancer. The sisters also participate in Teens for the Cure, a fund-raising activity run by the Philadelphia chapter of Komen for the Cure.

Gavi: "Being involved in some type of cancer activity makes you feel better. Cancer is a very uncontrollable disease. You feel you don't have any control of your diagnosis or your life or your health. When you participate in the teen program, you feel like you make a difference, have control over where the future of cancer is. You feel you can make a difference."

Mia: "I like what Gavi said: making people aware makes you feel better."

Hint, Hint: Not Everyone Is into Making Lemonade

Kaela, fourteen, whose stepdad died of prostate cancer: "Everyone says make lemonade out of lemons."

Meredith, sixteen, whose mom is a breast cancer survivor: "I didn't want to touch the lemons."

• •

14.5 Same Old You

I've been through this crazy ordeal, but I'm still the same old me...is that okay?!

Yes! There's no doubt that the experience has probably changed you a little bit, but that doesn't mean you have to reinvent yourself or become the next Mother Teresa.

You might ask yourself: "Am I shallow if I go back to being the same as I was before my parent had cancer?"

"I would say that, no, it doesn't mean you're shallow," says social worker Barbara Golby. "It also could be that how your experience has affected you will change with time. So maybe now as a teenager you're simply overwhelmed with relief that this is past you, and you're able to get on with the tasks of being a teenager. But when you reach more stable ground and safer territory, you'll be able to process a little more of what you just went through. It could be that teenagers just need to close the door for now."

Indeed, you may be at the point where you just don't want to hear anything more about cancer.

> "My mom piles on all this heavy stuff about cancer. You want her to stop, but she keeps on talking."
>
> —A teenage boy whose mom was treated for cancer and is doing well. But she still wants to talk about it.

Maya says: I literally would clam up every time cancer came up—whether it was "How's your mom doing now?" or just general cancer talk. It was a really visceral reaction. It wore off after a couple of years and now (almost a decade later) I'm 100 percent comfortable talking about it.

Marc says: We were so happy when Marsha's treatment ended. The kids surprised her by making a big banner to celebrate the end of chemo. Awww, even though it sometimes seemed they didn't really care what was going on, they really did! And then we kind of went back to being a semi-normal family, and we definitely had the normal parent-teen squabbles. Yet somehow, we seemed to all know that even though we didn't necessarily agree about a) curfews and b) the wisdom of sunbathing on the roof of the front porch, we all love each other a whole bunch and we aren't afraid to say it.

Perfectly Normal: It's fine to keep on keeping on. Don't block out the experience, but don't feel obligated to be a different person. You don't have to be more serious, responsible, independent. You can still just be you.

Angella's Story: Holding on to What You Believe

Angella was thirteen when her mother was diagnosed with breast cancer. Six years later, Mom is doing well. The experience has changed both mother and daughter.

Reflecting on her mother's transformation, Angella says, "She was previously too afraid to do anything social and would spend hours away from everyone on the computer. After the cancer she bustled around and joined workshops and cancer support groups and made friends. She became involved in life again. She became eager to rekindle her relationship with her children. She was completely remade for the better.

"As for myself, I was more conscious of cancer and still seek to look after myself in all the ways that may help me avoid cancer. I have connected with others who are going through [a parent's cancer] and helped them through it. I got involved with the Relay for Life.

"In a lot of ways, my 'new normal' isn't all that much different than my old normal. I'm more conscious of cancer, sure, but I still do the same things and have the same goals and am fighting for those with the same level of passion. I've seen major changes in my mother, but I haven't seen the same effect on myself. I've always been able to make it through things largely unscathed, and I suppose because I allowed myself to be completely honest with my feelings, and to acknowledge them as they were happening, I had the ability to retain my core beliefs.

"Cancer was simply an experience that cemented my thoughts: life is precious, and no price is too high to pay to preserve it. Love unconditionally, as much as you can, and treat every day as a gift. Seize it, use it, and make sure no one in your world goes to bed at night without knowing that you care. This life is far too short for hatred or fights. Disagreements may be necessary in order to progress, but why allow an argument to last longer than the one encounter it existed in? It simply isn't worth it."

• •

"In high school I had no idea how to cope with the intensity of the situation and turned to drugs. I was sent to an emotional-growth boarding school that brought me further away from my family's struggle. I am able to be so grateful for the sensitivities that developed within me through that process, because now I am able to heal others. Overall my mom's illness has been an incredible catalyst of change and growth in my life. But I still feel as though I have lived most of my life being a mother to my mother."

—Kellie, whose mom was diagnosed with lymphoma when
Kellie was nine and has been fighting cancer for twenty years

"Basically I wouldn't change that for anything because this helped me become not only a better person but see things differently, and I'm a better person because of it."

—Rob, seventeen, of Alabama, whose
mom is a breast cancer survivor

"The experience made me stronger in a way, emotionally. It's hard to explain. It just did. My faith has also gotten stronger. I'm not one for giving up hope, and neither is my mom."

—Luz of Virginia

14.6 Silver Linings

So how do we sum it all up? You may identify with some of the things in this book and not with others. Some may apply to you. Some may not apply at all. Maybe you really didn't change. Nothing is wrong with that.

But if we can generalize just this once, we will say that the cloud of cancer can have a silver lining if you look for it.

John of New Jersey remembers how his mom, after her diagnosis, would say: "It is what it is." That when something strikes you and it's out of your control, you just have to face it and move ahead as best you can, with the best attitude you can muster. That's the lesson he carries with him.

Cancer gave Molly, Samantha, and Lyndsey, three teen campers at Camp Kesem, a new view of family and of the power of love.

Lyndsey: "I used to hate to be around my mom. Now it doesn't bug me."

Samantha: "I tell my mom all the time that I love her."

Molly: "I think people take the words, 'I love you' for granted. I put 'love you' at the end of text messages [to my mom]. I want her to know I love her every second of the day."

Although maybe you don't have warm feelings toward your parents. Hey, that happens, too.

Then there are the kids who lost a parent to cancer. "Me and my dad were best friends," says Meghan, fourteen, of Ohio. "I lost my best friend."

Meghan's advice to anyone facing a parent's cancer: "You've just got to keep your head up, no matter what happens. Life is going to go on. Live life to the fullest. It's the most cliched thing..." But it's 110 percent true.

Oh yes, one more thing.

Meghan has learned the thing that we've all learned: cancer sucks!

"Cancer sucks. I want that written on every single wall all over the world. It's all I have to say about it. You never know what's going to happen. Nothing is set with cancer. CANCER SUCKS with a big exclamation point 100,000 times."

Who can disagree with that?

THE CAMP FOR KIDS COPING WITH A PARENT'S CANCER

Camp Kesem is not your usual summer camp. All the kids, who range in age from six to sixteen, have faced a parent's cancer. But the camp, which has forty-one locations, is not a therapeutic program. The sole agenda: have fun. The one-week stay is crammed with typical camp activities: sports, games, arts, and crafts.

Cancer is not part of the daily program but does sometimes come up in the course of the day or in evening bunk chats. And at each camp, there is one moment when all the campers do come together to talk about the bond that brings them together.

Here's what happened at an "empowerment" ceremony at the Camp Kesem just outside Charlottesville, Virginia, run by University of Virginia students.

There are seventy kids in the dining room, ages seven to sixteen. They are eating and talking and laughing, calling each other by their camp names—Sunshine, Freckles, Brazil, Boss, Eeyore. Some of the teenagers have paint on their clothes and hands and in their hair—it turns out the paint for a camp mural they've been working on isn't that easy to get off.

Then a miracle occurs. The kids become so quiet that the only sound you can hear is the ceiling fans, whirring over-head. It's time for the ceremony, held on Thursday night, just a couple days before the end of the weeklong camp.

At a regular camp, a camp-ending event might focus on

color war or conquering the great outdoors. Here the topics are intimate and emotional: cancer, parents, death. Anyone who wants to talk can come up and talk.

"I was really scared when my mom was diagnosed," a counselor confesses as she kicks off the program. "I didn't know what to do."

"At Camp Kesem everyone can understand some part of your feelings," a camper says. "I can forget all my troubles."

"My mom was diagnosed with breast cancer about five years ago," a boy says. "Her having cancer has been one of the toughest experiences of my life. Coming here let me forget about it. I met so many friends that actually know what it's like to have a parent with cancer."

A twelve-year-old boy comes up and talks about how so many kids have so many different experiences with cancer. "I haven't lost a parent," he says. "I'm sure some of you have. I'm not sure how you pull through. I don't know what I would do without my mom. Without her, my family would just crumble."

Lyndsey, who is sixteen and whose mom was diagnosed with stage 4 breast cancer in January, is the oldest camper to speak. "Everything gets put on me," she says. "I try to stay strong for my brothers. I wasn't excited to go here. I'm so caught up being mom to my brothers and my mom."

She didn't want to come to Camp Kesem and she hated it the first few days. But the camp lived up to its name—Kesem is Hebrew for magic. With nothing to do but have fun, Lyndsey had a change of heart. "I realized I really appreciate coming here," she says. "It's really going to be hard to go back home. I'm going to have to act twice my age again." Lyndsey begins to cry. She cries so hard she has to leave the room. A counselor goes out to comfort her.

A counselor talks about how kids come back each year and "face their fears." And they learn "we can lean on each other, we can learn from each other."

A girl who looks to be about twelve sums it all up: "Camp Kesem gives us all the chance to be normal kids again."

Then the kids walk down to the lakefront, still silent despite the emotions raging inside them. Each child has his or her hands on the shoulders of the person in front. It's called a "trust walk." They go down a winding pathway. Birds are chirping, cicadas are humming, and in the distance, you can hear the sounds of a camper who's sobbing.

The kids write their hopes and fears on small scraps of white paper. They toss the papers into a bonfire by the lake. "The fears will disintegrate into ash," a counselor says. "The hopes will rise up with the smoke." The twilight sky is full of blueberry-colored clouds with pearly white patches. Lush trees stand guard. The rite is very primitive, reflecting the primitive nature of cancer—an unruly and unexpected invader that knocks down doors and takes over lives.

But for this moment, cancer is not in charge. The kids are. They throw their fears and hopes into the fire, and they sing "Lean on Me" as the sky darkens and the smoke rises, carrying their hopes to the sky.

For more information on Camp Kesem,
see the Resources section on page 251.

In Their Own Words

Gilda's Club is a cancer support community named for *Saturday Night Live* comic Gilda Radner, who died of ovarian cancer in 1989. She wanted a place where anyone touched by cancer—patients, family, or friends—could receive emotional and social support as well as education. Clubs exist in cities across the United States.

Several of the clubs run an annual teen essay contest called "It's Always Something," one of Radner's catch phrases on *SNL*. Here are excerpts from essays from the Gilda's Club Seattle contest.

Editor's note: These are the original essays.

296 DAYS   MORGAN SMUCK

When I first heard my dad was sick it didn't really register. Dads are strong. Dads will always be there. Dads take care of kids. That was my world. My dad was first diagnosed with Myelodysplastic Syndrome which meant that he would receive blood transfusions and be a little tired. That fit into my world. There was a possibility that the syndrome would transition into Leukemia, but after having genetic work done, the absence of a particular gene indicated that it wouldn't. Just thirty days, and one blood test later, my dad had full blown Leukemia.

...At first, I didn't want my friends to know. I didn't want to be the one to tell them. I didn't want to have constant attention and sympathy from people who didn't know what I was dealing with or what I was going through. I didn't want my friends to ask me how I was feeling, or if I needed anything. Most of all, I didn't want people to tell me they were sorry, because I didn't know how to respond. I still don't. Then, a close friend of mine made phone calls to my friends telling them my situation. I was so relieved. People finally knew about my dad, and I was surrounded by silent support and unconditional love that never ceased.

Leukemia claimed my dad's life. But this is what I really want you to know about him. That at age 60 (he waited a long time to have me), he could still water ski on a single. He could out snow ski all of us in both speed and grace, and he sculled in a rowing shell. When we rode bikes together, he always pedaled up hills without stopping. When I was out of breath hiking up Tiger Mountain, he was a hundred steps ahead. My dad taught me to play tennis, helped me with math, and was always there. Before he had me, he served in Vietnam, summitted Mount Rainier, sailed to Tahiti, and restored a classic car. My dad loved to golf.

...Living through my father's battle with Leukemia taught me that life is too short and too precious for the typical or predictable. No matter how dedicated or organized we make ourselves, our typical, comfortable and predictable worlds can change in an instant.

I now look at my future through a vastly different lens, one that is in a sense broader, and at the same time more focused. Unlike most of my peers, I have been exposed to a much larger world that includes medicine, law, and the incredible compassion of professionals, friends and even strangers. I have learned how to support others, and how to accept the support of others in return.

I am now learning the importance of living an intentional life. I don't believe that I will ever get over the loss of my dad, but I am learning to live with it. After my dad's funeral, I received a letter from my high school English teacher that read, "Remember that your dad received what all fathers dream of: the love of kind and caring children. That is a love that he will always have." And that is what I hold on to.

HE TOOK ME TO THE DANCE   MARLENE PIERCE

It was my first high school dance. Homecoming '09, sophomore year. I hadn't planned on going, neither I nor my date were big on dancing. Yet, when I finally asked him to go, he said yes. I can assure you that it was the most memorable first date a girl could ever have. All dolled up in my dress with my hair curled, I put on heels to look taller next to my six foot escort. I walked out of my room to see my date standing there wearing a tux. Where my father found the tux I'll never know. "You ready to go Dad?" I asked. His answer was a quick yes.

My father was diagnosed with cancer the summer of '07. In the early stages, we were all hopeful that he would be the one to beat the odds. But cancer is a resilient foe, and soon it became clear that we might not have all the time we wanted. I found myself having to deal with the very real possibility that Daddy might not always be there. I worried that he might never see his grandchildren. That he'd never get the joy of interrogating the first boyfriend, and no doubt all who followed after, I brought home. That he might never walk me down the aisle. I remember crying in his arms, telling him all my worries, and I remember asking him to take me to homecoming.

The night of the dance, we were running an hour late. I didn't care though. I was the luckiest girl in Lake Stevens. I remember that as we got out of the car, the other late arrivals were all pointing and whispering, trying to figure out which football player I had brought to the dance. I remember my dad's chuckle as he overheard them. My dad had tumors up and down his spine, around his pelvis, and in the nerve bed of his foot. It's a miracle he could walk at all. But nothing stopped us from hobbling our way down that school aisle and slow dancing. We both cried as the music slowed and he said the three words all teenage girls dream of, "I love you."

We could only dance for forty minutes before we had to leave because of the pain from his tumors. But that forty minutes will last me a lifetime. It was my first dance at my wedding, it was my dad walking me down the aisle, his smile was that of a proud dad seeing his daughter graduate. We packed forty years into those forty minutes.

REMEMBER THIS   RACHEL CLARK

It was just over 8 months after my mom had been diagnosed with cancer, and the middle of November, when we prepared for a birthday gathering in the hospice for my mom. Seven years ago I spent that sunny morning at my friend's house, and we cut out dozens of bright red paper links that each guest could sign to join into a chain for her room. I arrived at the hospice excited to celebrate but my mom lay frail and very still, breathing heavily in a bed surrounded by humming machines. The party was cancelled. I knew, everyone knew, that this was it, that this birthday candle was beginning to flicker and dim. I was asked to go stand by her bed and talk to her, and was told that though she could not respond, she could hear my voice. There is no way to prepare for the last words you can say to your mom.

ROLLER COASTER   GUY T. SIMPSON, III

There is a loud metallic *clack-clack-clack* as the roller coaster car begins to climb to its dizzying apex of the first perilously high hill on the track, followed by a moment of fear and apprehension as the track drops into the far distance below, and with a rush of air and the chorus of screams the car plummets downward and your stomach hangs in the balance. When a son learns that their beautiful, supportive mother who has always been there for him has been diagnosed with this disease called cancer, that strikes fear into so many, the only way I can describe it that makes any sense at all, is a roller coaster. The past year and a half has been a constant deluge of fear, apprehension, unconditional love, and uncertainty for my family and I know we will never be the same. In October of 2009 my mother went in to the doctor to get her abdominal pain checked and came away with a diagnosis of colon cancer. She had emergency surgery to remove the tumors from her colon and lumps from her ovaries.

That week, the amusement ride conductor in my life said, "Keep your arms and legs inside the car, I hope you enjoy the ride."

clack-clack-clack

My two older sisters, who were in their freshmen and sophomore years of college respectfully, and I watched our strong, independent mother waste away little by little and there was nothing we could do to help her. It was so unfair to have this happen, there was no history of colon cancer in my mom's family, and she was so healthy and vital. My mother started chemotherapy right before Christmas and she handled it like a trooper, the regimen did put her in the hospital a couple times in the New Year as she got weaker. The roller coaster was whizzing at a rapid pace by then, but there was another monstrous hill looming on the horizon.

clack-clack-clack

Things changed when she started radiation. It completely broke her down and she spent the next month and a half in the hospital. Throughout it all, my father worked day and night to try to make our lives normal. He did his best to continue working as a middle school teacher and coach, while still finding time to prepare the meals, do our laundry, take us shopping and help us with our homework but it wore him thin doing all those things and spending time in the hospital visiting Mom till the wee hours of the night. We would do our best to go to school and work during the day and then rush off to the hospital to spend time with Mom, trying to make the most out of each visit. Each of us handled the twists and turns of the roller coaster track in our own unique ways. My dad has long been my role model, and my hero. He rose up to a new level beyond those titles during our early time on the roller coaster. He stayed strong and showed very little emotion towards us or Mom. As a child he was told by his uncle that crying made it hurt worse. He was thirteen when his uncle died. He has never cried for the loss of his uncle, and he did his best to hold it all together despite his own worries and fears for our benefit.

He was a rock that we all relied on in the stormy seas. He never, ever gave up on my mom. He kept telling her to fight. He kept reminding her how much he loved her and how much we all needed her. Dad handled Mom's cancer by stepping up and taking care of the family. My mom calls him her knight in shining armor, always there to protect her. His quirky sense of humor kept us going on some very dark days. He teased Mom about the Power Port her surgeon installed on the middle of her chest, saying she was just like Ironman. It was his love and support that kept us together and held us on the track as we rocketed through loops and dangerous obstacles.

My oldest sister, Taylor, remained very stoic through it all. As an intellectual, she researched it and then she simply said, "It's only cancer, it's beatable, and it won't kill you." She never outwardly thought twice about it. She never really shared with us how much she was hurting inside or how scared she truly was. However, the stress she was feeling became evident one day when she called my mom while she was in the hospital and cried because she could not find a parking space in the hospital parking lot. My mom talked with the nurse and they figured out a place for Taylor to park. Her endless sobbing actually made my mom laugh and it made my mom feel good that she could help her daughter, even from her hospital bed. Taylor dealt with my mother's illness by trying to avoid it and focus on other things; she still claims she never once doubted that Mom would win her battle with cancer.

My other sister, Katie, had the hardest time. Katie has wanted to be a doctor since third grade. So she was very supportive of Mom through this whole roller coaster ride. She was in the office when my mother got the news that she had cancer. Katie and Mom sat in the doctor's office and simply cried. I think Mom sent the rest of us a text message telling us it was not good news. Katie was with Mom and Dad for almost everything, her first CT scan, her first labs, her first consult with the surgeon and the oncologist, and she was there for Mom when Dad could not be. I look back on it now and am so glad that Mom did not have to go through all of that alone; she needed one of us there by her side.

Katie would be the one to shuttle Mom to her radiation appointments as Mom could not drive as she got weaker and weaker. Katie was also the one that cleaned up the throw up and the diarrhea messes without ever complaining. There was one time when my mom had an incontinent bowel accident and her clothes were covered in yuck. Mom just stood there and cried not knowing what to do, but Katie jumped in, put two garbage bags over Mom's feet and walked her into the shower. Katie told Mom that it would be their little secret as she cleaned up the mess. Katie managed to get through Mom's struggle by being her caretaker and finding oncology as her first choice when she goes off to medical school.

I struggled with my mother's diagnosis in my own way. My mom kept asking me how I felt and I kept silent. I did not talk about it. Academically I faltered, losing focus in many of my classes and falling hopelessly behind in my pre-calculus class, drowning in my Advanced Placement courses. Athletically I struggled due to my lack of focus. Socially I was at a new school, having transferred just months before from Rainier to Yelm, and found myself adrift in a sea of unfamiliar faces. My mother's cancer buried me so deep I could not see daylight anymore.

Roller coasters are supposed to be fun, a thrill ride, but for me this one was anything but that. I had been relying on my online social network, my friends from my old school, and the few new friends I had made at Yelm to express my feelings about my mother. I was posting on Facebook to my friends about how sick my mother was, how horrible it was to deal with a loved one fighting cancer, and how scared I was that I might actually lose my mother. It was not until my dad set up a Facebook account for my mother so that she would have something to do as she sat during her pain ridden days. My mom, of course, friended my sisters and I. In time, my mom saw my Facebook postings which read like a painful open diary of my account with her cancer diagnosis, and we were finally able to talk. I told her that it is not fair that a child has to think about losing a parent before I had even really begun to live.

It was during this time that we found how physically challenging it was for my mom to comfort me. She used to hold her baby boy close to her heart but now that I am six feet eight inches tall it is not so easy. It sounds kind of silly but I found it was easier to text her or email her sometimes as it was hard to sit and talk about how I was feeling. I was trying to stay strong like my hero, my dad. But in the end I did not do either very well. I dealt with my mom's cancer and the possibility of losing her by talking to others first through the emotionless safety of the Internet.

A family cancer diagnosis truly is like a roller coaster, with its highs and lows. We have experienced a slew of frightening times, only to find ourselves in the midst of unconditional love from our parents, or the growing apprehension for what twist or turn might lay ahead on the course, just out of sight.

I know that everybody deals with stress in different ways. This past year has tested my family to the very core. Some say that cancer can divide a family. We are fortunate; colon cancer brought my family even closer together, but one truth seems to stand out after all of this. Once you board the roller coaster of a cancer diagnosis, you can never get off, the ride just continues, and all you can do is learn to love your time together and enjoy the special hidden moments that happen along the way.

As for my mother, *clack-clack-clack,* Mom's last CT scan shows no active cancer in her colon—thank God—but, she has a spot on her lung that we are watching very closely. Cancer has taught us to appreciate life, to stop and smell the roses when we had been used to living life in the fast lane. As a family, we try to spend more time together and cherish the memories we have created. Individually, we are beginning to heal. My father and I even shared a long, cathartic tearful hug. I know I will never take my family for granted. My sisters and parents are too important to me. As I near the end of my high school career, my mother's cancer now has given me focus. Like my sister before me, I too, have decided to pursue the study of medicine in college because of this ordeal.

COFFEE, BEDPANS, REHEARSALS & YOU, DADDY   SYDNEY KASER

I am ashamed of how I feel and I'm not afraid to admit it. I blush at the thought of what I want. The thought of what I pray to God for every single day. Pray to the God that I don't think exists; but I do it anyway. I won't pretend that I'm OK. I won't tell you I'm fine when I know you know I'm not. I won't smile just to shrug you off. I won't tell you lies just to get you off my back. This is my reality and you're welcome to it. My father has leukemia. Yes. I said it. It doesn't make it any less real or any better. It just is.

YOU AND I   ANONYMOUS

Dear Mom,

Because of you it only takes that one word to hit me hard. Cancer. It stops the blood running through my veins. It stops the world that's going on around me. I stop to concentrate on what this word means to me, to you, and to others. Yet I do not have a definition of it in my head. Is it some kind of sickness that could ruin us? Or is it something that will be healed like my broken nose during soccer season?

I googled the word Cancer for days, checked it out on health sites, but still I don't have a clear understanding of what it is. The dictionary tells me: a disease caused by an uncontrolled division of abnormal cells in a part of the body. But I think cancer has many more meanings than the counts of cells in your body. Cancer means the number of soccer games you'll actually be able to attend this year, how many nights you'll be up with me helping me fix our damn printer for a school project due the next day yet again, or even how many more lectures I'll receive from you this year about what's right and what's wrong.

It's been just a near 5 months since you've been diagnosed with Cancer, and not once have we talked about it. I push it aside, like it's no big deal and you'll get through it, like you do with everything else. I'm in denial to put it the simple way.

Talking about problems that I'm dealing with or facing has never been the easiest. I've always been a bigger help when we discussed what color shoes you should wear to your function that night, rather than the subject of Cancer. I can't comfort you and tell you everything's ok, because it's not. And I sure as hell can't tell you what I'm thinking because I can't even control my own thoughts anymore.

When you left your clumps of beautiful golden hair on the bathroom counter I simply got a Kleenex tissue and covered them up, and went on to doing my own business. When people would ask me where my mom was today, I put a smile on my face and told them 'The Hospital' with no further explanation just like everything was peachy.

Every night, when reality hits, I cry for you. It's sometimes hard waking up to a puffy face and little tears. In my own selfish matter I think about myself sometimes. I ask myself the big question: what's going to happen to me if something bad happens to you?

If we were your average family we could tell everyone that I'll be just fine, living with my dad and my siblings, continuing to live life without you, but we're not. We're a family of two, just you and I. Don't get me wrong and think I'm blaming you for the summer love you shared with a man in Istanbul, Turkey. I wouldn't have asked for life any other way than just the two of us. Although it still comes down to the question: what's going to happen to me? Am I going to live with my Grandma who's soon reaching 80? Am I being shipped off to my "Dad" that I have no recollection of? Will I live with my aunt who loves her dogs more than anyone else she knows? Or will I be stuck living with my other aunt that already has 2 kids and struggles to keep her house and almost lost it a numerous amount of times?

I hope this decision will never have to be made, and the answer will always be YOU. You're the one I will live with. You're the one that will get through this and live to tell the story. You'll be the one that will help me with my heartbreaks soon to come. You'll teach me everything I need to know about these next 4 years of high school. Although no matter what happens I know one place you'll always be. My heart.

Love,
Me

FOR YOU, DADDY   CAROLINE MIN

Cancer. The one word that causes everyone to shudder. I never thought I would see anyone deal with such a horrifying disease, let alone anyone from my family. Cancer was supposed to be an illness that was only shown on television or read about in books: not something that would affect me personally. But I know I'm not alone. Millions of people have had to suffer the same pain I have, and I wish to support all those who are currently undergoing the dreadful tribulations of this atrocious disease. As for now, I am forced to face reality myself. Only 53 days until a year has passed. Only 53 days until I will have to overcome my fear of being in total remembrance of the day my life was completely altered. Only 53 days. It truly is amazing how fast time flies.

That fateful day, I remember it vividly. I doubt that the image will ever vanish from my thoughts. The day my world came crashing down on me. March 25th, 2008. I came home to my crying mother who was accompanied by a hospice worker. Although this was uncommon, I did not stop to think of what was occurring; instead, I as a naive and foolish child went upstairs to go about my daily tasks. After a while, I came down as my mother called me; unaware of the significance of the words I was about to hear, I simply stared as I watched my mom break down. What I heard next created an indescribable feeling deep within me, the words no one wants to hear. Essentially, it all came down to this: "It seems as if your dad only has a week or so left to live..."

Although this may seem implausible, these words hit me hard for one reason: for the past two years, I had never thought that I would ever lose my dad. My faith in God surpassed all the doubts that had ever even thought to cross my mind. Despite my mother's cautions to "be prepared" in case it did happen, I never stopped to think of the reality of the situation. My dad, the man who seemed to have no fears or weaknesses. My dad, the man who always made all those around him laugh. My dad, the man who constantly teased me with a smile on his face. My dad, the man who no one seemed to be able to dislike. My dad, my dad, my dad…it simply did not click.

Until this moment. I hate crying in front of my mom, let alone a complete stranger, so I left to talk to my dad himself. When I came to him, I realized then how true the actuality of the circumstances was. Tears rolling down my face, I stared at my one and only daddy. He was now in a completely different state from what he had used to be. The once lively and active man I knew was now confined to a bed, unable to do anything alone. He had become another child, a child who could not walk, a child with a diaper because he could not go to the bathroom, a child who rarely talked, a child who must be fed and cleaned by another person. Although it may seem childish, for some reason, I rarely say the words "I love you." However, for the first time in a long time, I stared at my dad with tears streaming down my cheek, and I said the three most powerful words known to humans, "Daddy, I love you…"

MY MOM MACON ABERNATHY

"Guys, come in here! Your mom and I need to share something with you." That cry of my Dad is now just a faint whisper of my memory. It had been nearly seven years since my Mom was diagnosed with breast cancer. So many highs and lows happened over those seven years; I can't express in words the joy and overwhelming feeling of thanks to God that the news of a tumor eradication can bring. Nor can I speak of the sinking sorrow that follows the discovery that the cancer has spread. Just as hard to describe is the experience of seeing God's delivering hand through all of my Mom's trials. All of the chemotherapy and radiation treatments I went to with her; all of the walks we went on as part of her training for the Avon 3-Day; all of these memories, and many more I now cherish as my tie to my Mom's amazing life, love and strength.

The Parents' Guide

Welcome to parental guidance. The first question you may be asking yourself is: how hard is it to raise teens while coping with cancer? And the answer, from someone who knows all too well: very hard.

Wendy Harpham, a physician and mother of three, was diagnosed with non-Hodgkins lymphoma when her children were one, three, and five. She has had seven recurrences over the years, so she knows what it's like to have youngsters of different ages during cancer treatment.

People felt sorry for her when her kids were little. Little kids are so needy. And the diapers! Actually, that wasn't so bad, Harpham recalls. "It was pretty straightforward because their world revolved around us."

Teenage children are much more challenging. "Under the best of circumstances, parenting a teen is physically and emotionally expensive," she explains. "The task of teens is to separate from the nuclear family, to test out their independence. The parents' job is to be vigilant about how their kids are testing the boundaries. And teens are notorious for being mercurial, self-centered, impulsive, and at times irrational."

Yikes! But Harpham and her family have all survived cancer's blows. She came to the realization that "I don't have to be perfect. You do the best you can do." You can forgive each other—and forgive yourself—when you mess up. And then you move forward.

Today, she says, "My kids are twenty-two, twenty-four, and twenty-six. They are so resilient, so reality-based, so easy to forgive, so ready to embrace today."

"Without a doubt," she sums up, "I would never call my cancer a gift. But facing my illness made me a much better mother."

As you read this guide, you'll find sections that relate to the chapters for teens in this book. Each chapter will be referenced so that you can flip back to it if you want.

• •

A Dozen Commandments for Parents

Okay, Mom and Dad, you have a lot on your plate. One of you has cancer. The other one is a cancer caregiver. And both of you are parents of at least one teenager, or else you wouldn't be reading this book.

One thing we will repeatedly say is that every kid is different, every family is different. So the rule is: there's no one-size-fits-all advice. But there are exceptions to every rule. Here are twelve commandments that should pretty much hold true.

1. Communicate! News bulletins about the cancer and treatment must be delivered even if the teen is not asking for details.

2. "Don't check out of parenting," says social worker Seth Berkowitz. Teens still need you to be the parent.

3. Don't hide bad news. They'll figure it out from the look on your face—or else be really ticked off that you didn't let them know how serious things are.

4. Don't make them talk if they don't want to. Respect your (sometimes moody) adolescent's mood.

5. Worry if your teen does anything that would normally make you worry—avoiding friends, experimenting with risky business, doing badly in school.

6. Say thank you for extra chores handled. And say

it again. And again. You can't imagine how much it means to a teen. Maybe even throw in a reward.

7. If they want to go with you to an appointment, let them.

8. If they apologize for saying something cruel, accept the apology! Be grateful for it. It is not easy for teens to apologize (or adults either, for that matter). Do not say, "That was a really thoughtless thing you said earlier." If you say that, you'll never get another "I'm sorry."

9. Designate a go-to adult, if you can, for moments when you're not available or when your kid might need an adult confidant. An aunt, uncle, grandparent, neighbor— anyone your teen has a close relationship with.

10. Remember: video games can help teens cope with stress. So can exercise, watching stupid movies, hanging with friends, going to the mall, and listening to music you personally can't stand!

11. You don't have to be upbeat 100 percent of the time. Optimism may make life more enjoyable but it does not cure cancer. It's okay to admit to your kids that sometimes you feel down.

12. Don't forget to tell your teens, "I love you." Even on a day when you're really mad at them!

• •

WHEN DO YOU TELL THEM?

Parents, if you're just not emotionally capable of delivering the news about a cancer diagnosis on the day you get it, well then, take a day. Or maybe even a week. Just don't wait forever. And at the outset and throughout the months of treatment, you have to determine what your kids need to know and when they need to know it.

For example, if you're waiting for test results and are kind of jumpy, you don't need to tell your kids and make them jumpy, too. It's okay to wait for the results, then share.

If you're feeling that this is all Just Too Much, social worker Seth Berkowitz suggests you look for expert help. A cancer center or support organization might have a staff social worker or child life specialist who would be willing to meet with you and the kids and answer questions. (The Resources in Appendix D offer some possible places to start.) Berkowitz advises: "It's okay to say, 'I have cancer; this is the kind. I made an appointment for us to go and learn more about it together.'"

(For related material for teens, go to Chapter 1.)

WHAT DO YOU TELL THEM?

You may *think* you know exactly what your teenager needs in terms of information. The real question is: what does your teenager need to know?

"It's easy for people who have big hearts to feel they know what they would want if they were in their child's situation," says psychiatrist Paula Rauch. "But what are the child's needs?"

Here's how to find out: ask them.

Let's say the doctors are in favor of a bone marrow transplant, in which a donor provides healthy cells that are inserted into the patient's bloodstream or the patient's own marrow is harvested for a transplant. Tell the kids why this procedure is being recommended and what the outlook is.

But don't just tell them and figure you've done your job. The next day you might inquire: "This discussion we had about the bone marrow transplant—did I tell you too much or too little?"

Some children will want you to curb your information-giving. "If your child says, 'Talking about this with you is not helpful to me,'" says Paula Rauch, "it's really important to respect that."

Then there is the child who doesn't want to hear anything. It is still important to deliver any breaking news about the cancer. Rauch suggests that you could try saying something like: "You might hear me talking about this with someone else, so here's what you might hear." Or you and your spouse might just talk about medical concerns when the kids are around. Even if you think they've tuned you out, they're probably listening.

Keep in mind that your child may be inconsistent from day to day. "One day your adolescent is incredibly moody and won't say a word to you," says psychologist Anne Coscarelli, "and the next moment, you're busy doing something else and they come in and chat your ear off. It's important to realize that, with adolescents, you don't always pick the time or place where the conversation is going to take place. But it's good to have the presence of mind to make it a priority to listen when they do start talking to you. You might not get another shot for a while."

Physician and cancer survivor Wendy Harpham has juggled the needs of a kid who thrives on information and another who wants the bare minimum.

"The essential question," she says, "is what information does the child need to deal with his or her world? I don't think a child needs to know how much pain a parent is in to deal with his or her world unless the pain is affecting what the parent says or does."

And Harpham has learned that you don't have to pretend to know it all: "One statement I find very helpful is: 'It's always a work in progress.'"

Marc says: Some kids won't ask questions. Some will ask yes-or-no questions. And some of them may appear to be studying for medical school.

So your kid might ask a question you don't know how to answer. That's nothing to be embarrassed about. (Take it from me, a guy who didn't know the difference between chemotherapy and radiation when my wife started treatment.)

If the question is a medical one and you're stumped, oncology social worker Jill Taylor-Brown suggests saying to your teenager: "That's a really good question. I'm going to see the doctor next Thursday. I'll ask."

And sometimes there are no answers. That's just the way cancer is.

The way to find out how you're doing on the information front is to ask your teens: are we telling you everything you need to know? Do you have questions? Or is this too much information? Or maybe if you're not into talking about it, we could write the information in a note so you can read it in private when you're ready.

(Check out Chapter 3, section 3.4 in the teen section for ways to keep the dialogue open with your teenager.)

Words of Wisdom:
"Our guiding principle was to say it and to say it clearly and straightforwardly, without hedging, without trying to whitewash it. To say what we know, to say it simply. The tightrope is between giving the information we feel needs to be given and not giving more information than is necessary."

—Psychologist Richard Ogden, father of three, whose wife was diagnosed with metastatic breast cancer and died of the disease

Helping Your Teenager Cope

You're trying to cope with cancer. But you have another parental task: helping your kids deal.

Reassure them. Maybe they're afraid you'll die. They might have picked up the fear from you, or maybe they just instinctively fear this insidious disease. One way to help your kids get over some of their fears is to mention people who are survivors. People in the public eye, like Olympic gymnast Shannon Miller and actress Christina Applegate. Or just people you know from your circle of family members and friends and neighbors. Recognizing that there are many cancer survivors can make the word "cancer" seem a little less overwhelming.

Tune in. Sometimes you are oblivious to what your teenager is thinking. That's understandable. "When there's a sick family member, adolescents get pushed to the side a lot of the time," says oncology counselor Shara Sosa. "Parents and other adult caregivers think little ones need so much more attention. I always tell people, kids don't ever get old enough that they don't need you. They need you more in adolescence."

Don't overburden them. It's tempting to lean on teens. But try not to use them to pick up all the chores you can't handle. "Parents need to have the wisdom to recognize that teenagers still need their own time," says social worker Bunty Anderson. "They can't suddenly be expected to be home from school at four and skipping basketball because the snow needs to be shoveled." Hiring help, if you can afford it, or accepting help from family and friends "is much smarter than to heap it all on the kids."

Defuse tensions. Conflict happens without cancer in the house. If parent-teen arguments are escalating, Anderson suggests saying something like: "Of course, we're all feeling upset about Dad being sick. I think that's why everybody's temper is short. But we need to be thoughtful about how we spend our time together. We need to put our energy into things that are life giving and not sucking all of us dry because who wants to fight all the time?"

Make together time. Don Fisher remembers that when his wife was going through cancer treatment but feeling okay, the family would keep up their habit of having dinner with the kids. "We would watch movies together," he adds. "We kept a fairly regular life."

If you can, give your kids permission to invite friends over. Tell them if certain times are off limits—say, the days right after chemo. If Mom or Dad bounces back from chemo after a week or so, tell the kids, "This is a good week to have friends over."

Above all, Mom and Dad, try not to take anything personally—even if your teen is embarrassed about the way you look during cancer. "Don't feel angry or bad," says child life specialist Kathleen McCue. "And don't say, 'I'm so sorry.'" You don't have to apologize to the kid for your appearance. You might say, "I really am the same person inside but I know the way I look on the outside is important. Until I look more like my old self, I'll skip your basketball games. But I want the play by play, and ask a friend to make a video, too."

Mom or Dad, you are now officially a candidate for sainthood. You've let your teen know you are still interested in his or her life, and you've acknowledged that your changed appearance is hard for them. "That's a very generous and well-adjusted parent," McCue says.

(For ideas to help teens deal with how cancer changes things and develop coping skills, go to Chapters 4 and 6.)

Is Your Teen Suddenly Becoming the Parent?

Let's say that you notice your teenager is exhibiting symptoms of parentification: acting more like a parent than a big brother or sister to younger siblings, spending too much time at home, taking on too many chores. Let the teen know you appreciate the help. But then say: relax a bit, have some fun, leave the dishes for me.

P.S.: Don't forget to say thank you for whatever help they provide.

Teens may feel "angry that they have to take over everything and nobody appreciates that they're doing so much more than they used to do," says psychiatrist Karen Weihs. Saying thank you makes a difference. It may sound like a little thing, and you may think you've thanked your teenager a gazillion times. Maybe you haven't even thanked them once because you're feeling overwhelmed, too.

(For more on parentification from the teen perspective, go to Chapter 5.)

IS YOUR TEEN AT RISK FOR RISKY BUSINESS?

Elissa Bantug, a teen rebel when her mother was diagnosed with breast cancer (see section 7.2), now advises cancer patients on how to cope after treatment ends. She tells cancer patients: "Put your own needs first." But for patients who are parents, she stresses that they should not put their kids' needs on the back burner.

Bantug's recommendations:

Be there. The storm of cancer can sweep you away from parental duties. You must continue to be a parent, especially if you worry that your teens are engaging in risky behavior. If you can't be there, make sure another family member or good family friend is. "It has been my experience that if you do not care for your kids," Bantug says, "they will find someone (or something) else that will."

Learn to listen. Let your kids know they can ask questions and tell you if they're afraid. Don't just answer with clichés or dismiss their concerns. Tune into what they're saying and answer their questions honestly.

Set clear expectations. Just because Mom or Dad is sick doesn't mean grades can drop or chores are no longer required. Be consistent with your rules so your teens know what you expect from them.

Try to involve them. Yes, it's okay to ask them to pitch in. Maybe that means serving as sous chef when you're trying to get meals prepared for the week ahead, or picking up a younger sibling at a friend's house. "But I caution parents that there's a fine line," Bantug says. "Kids still need to be kids and not feel overburdened."

Have fun. Family movies night or game night sound hokey

but could be a nice way for everyone to share upbeat moments during the months of treatment. Or you can ask a neighbor to help plan a fun activity for your teen.

Get to know your child's friends. The turmoil of cancer might cause your teen to seek new friends. If you don't like the friends, you might want to say, "I don't want you going out with [insert friend's name here]." "That can often backfire," observes Bantug. And in the cell phone era, your kid can tell you she's one place and really be someplace else. "I sometimes advise parents that if you don't like your child's friends, insist that the friends hang out at your house where at least you know they will be properly supervised."

Look to the future. Let teens know you understand how frustrating all of the changes in the household are. Give them a guesstimate of how long it will take before treatment ends and Mom or Dad may feel better. Saying something like, "By next spring I should be well enough to come to your soccer games again," lets teens know that the stresses of active treatment will not last forever.

(Check out Chapter 7 for stories of how some teens who got into risky business turned their lives around.)

When the News Isn't So Positive

How do you tell your kids that you're not so optimistic at a particular moment?

Let's say some news came from the doctor and it's not encouraging. Psychiatrist Paula Rauch suggests you might say, "We're disappointed and upset. We wanted the news to be different."

Or maybe you just hit a low ebb in the inevitable ups and downs of treatment. "Say it's normal for people to have ups and downs in the day," Rauch recommends. Tell the kids: "You're catching me at a moment when I feel really tired and down. One thing I know about myself is that sometimes I have really blue afternoons but later that day, or the next day, I feel much better." Then you might share your plan for how you get to a better frame of mind. Maybe that means taking a shower or bath, going for a walk, or watching a favorite funny movie.

Don't dump all your negative feelings on your teenager. "If a parent feels continuously down and feels they need to use their child as the person to talk about how upset they are, how depressed they are, how unbearable this all is, that ought to be a sign to the parent that they need help from another grown-up," Paula Rauch says.

It's also fine for parents to use the comments of doctors to put things in perspective. Maybe you might say to your kids, "My doctors feel really optimistic about being able to make the cancer go away, so even though sometimes you see me down or discouraged, you should just know I'm a lot more discouraged than my doctors are."

If your child asks, "Will you die?" you can say, "I hope not." But you know there's a possibility that you will. So you can tell your teen: "I want you to know that many people in your life love you, and they will continue to be in your life if I die."

You can try to strengthen those relationships. If it's time to shop for a prom dress, invite Cousin Ari, who has incredibly good fashion sense. If your teen is struggling with a college essay, suggest that Aunt Arlene, the editor, would be the perfect person to bounce ideas off.

"It's often quite comforting to the parent to think that the child will have someone in certain arenas," psychiatrist Paula Rauch says. "And it gives the child the message that this is something the parent has sanctioned"—that turning to another family member for support is not being disloyal to the parent suffering from cancer.

(Go to Chapter 12 to find suggestions for teens whose parents face a tough diagnosis.)

Telling the School: Who to Talk To

It's probably a safe bet that you don't want to set up a summit meeting with your teen's seven teachers. You've got enough worries without adding "meeting scheduler" to the to-do list.

Try starting with the guidance counselor assigned to your child, suggests school psychologist Ricia Weiner. In secondary school, kids often have the same counselor each year. Thus, the counselor should have met with your child from time to time.

Your teen may be fine with that. Or he or she may say, "I don't like my guidance counselor."

"We don't always get along with everybody," admits school social worker Melissa Ford. "And that's okay. What's most important is that teens find someone they are comfortable with." And whatever the reason behind a rocky counselor-student rapport, that relationship could turn around in the face of a cancer crisis.

Other possible points of contact: the school social worker or psychologist, if there is one on staff. Or even a favorite teacher or coach.

"The faculty at my high school was extremely supportive of me and my family," remembers Callie, whose mom was diagnosed with pancreatic cancer ten years ago, when Callie was seventeen, and is still alive today. "My guidance counselor was a wonderful person to talk to."

Words of Wisdom:
"We ask the parents to write something to share with the teachers so we're not sharing things they don't want us to or saying it in a way they don't want. Type up an email and send it to us. We're happy to forward it to everybody."

—School psychologist Ricia Weiner

You and your teen should talk about how much information you want the school to have. Maybe just the fact that there's been a cancer diagnosis and that treatment will proceed over the next six months or so is enough. Or you might want to go into more detail if this is a complicated cancer scenario.

That email should address head-on the burning question: how does your teen want to handle all this? Such as:

- It's okay to share with teachers but make sure they do not mention my cancer in class.
- It is all right to ask my daughter privately, after class, how she is doing.
- Please let the guidance counselor know of issues with grades or classroom behavior, and the counselor will contact her father and me.

(For more suggestions on how to deal with your teen's school, go to Chapter 10.)

HELP WITH FRIENDS

If you're worried that your child doesn't have someone close at school to confide in, you can help find someone. If your teenager has somebody who would be a good candidate for a confidant—an uncle, a rec league coach, her best friend's mom—you can ask that person: would you be the go-to person for my kid? If the answer is yes, tell your teenager: if you have any questions, if we're not around because we're at the doctor's office, or I'm at work and Dad is home sleeping after chemo, or whatever...call this person.

If a teen is talking to an outside adult, the ground rules are usually that the discussions are confidential. Most of the time, that's fine.

"The parent knows the child has an outlet, a place to talk about fears. You do want to respect the teenager's privacy and let them do some independent problem solving," says child life specialist Kathleen McCue.

What if your teen is not talking to you at all, and you have no clue what's up? And what if that teen raises an issue with the confidant that the parents really, truly should know about? The parents might tell both the teen and the confidant: "If something is really wrong, we expect to hear about it."

(Chapter 9 provides advice for teens on how to tell their friends and deal with changes in friendships after a parent is diagnosed with cancer.)

Therapy

Suppose you're worried about your teenager. Gabe is shut up in his room and never comes out, not even to hang with his buddies. Rosie used to get all A's, but now her grades are plummeting and she seems worried all the time. Henry disappears on weekends and smells of liquor when he finally does come home.

These are the kinds of issues that would make a parent worry under any circumstances. And the fact that you are devoting your energies to dealing with cancer doesn't mean you can afford to ignore the warning signs.

"The first rule of thumb," says psychiatrist Paula Rauch, "is that if nobody in the family were sick and you were seeing the same constellation of mood and behavior, would you seek help?"

Even in the best of times, parents aren't always sure when to seek help. "It's a complicated question for parents," Rauch

Words of Wisdom:

"One of the biggest determining factors in therapy is whether the person likes their therapist," says social worker Seth Berkowitz. He suggests that parents might try something like this: "Let's pick two or three therapists and meet with them and see if one of them is someone you'd like to talk to, that you feel comfortable with. Let's interview a couple of people together." And tell your teen that if he doesn't like any of them, he can tell you so.

says. "I always say people are more clear about when to bring their car in to be fixed—when it makes knocking and pinging noises. When the teenager is making knocking and pinging noises, parents are less quick to get a consultation."

The parents might start by consulting with a counselor—perhaps a school counselor, or a child psychologist or psychiatrist. You might also seek out a specialist. "There's a branch of family therapy called medical family therapy," says psychologist Barry J. Jacobs. "One thing we do is help families as a whole, especially children, deal with chronic or life-threatening illness in the family."

If you think a therapist would help your teen, you then have to convince the teen that seeing a therapist is worthwhile. And that might be like trying to convince your pet kitty to jump into the ocean.

Survival Tip: When there's not a will, there's not a way. "If you don't want to come to see me, you'll find a way to not be here," psychologist Barry J. Jacobs has found. Sure, the parent might require the teenager to go to a session or two. "But the child has to buy into it," says Jacobs. "There has to be some value. And it has to be not stigmatizing to come."

"I was not open to talking to anyone specialized. I wanted to keep to myself. I didn't want to talk to anyone, especially someone assigned to me, like a therapist."
—Morgan of Seattle, whose dad was diagnosed with cancer when she was a teenager and died within a year

Therapists aren't miracle workers. Some kids see a therapist and don't find it helpful.

Yet sometimes they really, really do.

As a last resort, play the guilt card. Social worker Sara Goldberger suggests: "You might say: 'It would help me to know that you were doing this. If you won't do it for yourself, do it for me.'"

Survival Tip: Parents, ask your cancer doc or a hospital with a cancer center to recommend a therapist. You can also approach a cancer support organization in town or even your kid's school (if your kid is okay with you talking to a counselor for suggestions).

(For more on how teens can seek help beyond their friends and family, go to Chapter 11.)

When the Outlook Is Grim

Cancer can force parents to consider the outcome that no one wants to face. That, as one parent put it about his wife's condition, "Things have gone south."

In another generation, the matter of a parent's impending death often wasn't discussed at all. Psychologist Barry J. Jacobs remembers what it was like in the early 1970s, when he was a teen and his dad was dying of cancer. "My parents were not open at all. It was back in the dark ages when people didn't talk about the 'c' word."

Teens now have far more access to information than back when Jacobs was a teenager. But they can't figure out everything by going online.

"What I would recommend to parents is to give their child a very basic outline of what's going on and asking the child how much they want to know, how much detail," says Jacobs. That's critical when the parent with cancer is likely to succumb to the disease. The teenager is almost certainly not going to come to you and say, "What's going to happen?"

So it's up to you to take the lead, to help your teens deal with the reality that Mom or Dad might die and to talk about how that death will affect the family. Here are some things to think about if you're in that position.

MAKING MEMORIES: THE PARENT'S PERSPECTIVE

You may wonder what kind of memories your teen will have of you. Don't just wonder. You can be part of the making of memories. If you can bear to sit for a video, make a tape recording, or write a letter, it could mean the world to your child. "When teens read legacy documents, videos, letters, they treasure them," says social worker Jill Taylor-Brown.

For those who do want to write a letter to their kids, Taylor-Brown warns not to be too bossy with statements like study hard, don't do drugs, and so on. "That can be a burden on the teen," she notes. Messages of love, memories and stories, she says, are better to share.

There is a note of caution for both parent and teen. When Richard Ogden's wife knew that her cancer would be terminal, she chose not to write letters to her three daughters. "She had more trust in their memory of her," says Ogden, "than in a letter that might be too prescriptive or too confining."

"Nobody's saying you shouldn't write a letter," he adds. But think carefully about what you want to write.

WHO GETS WHAT?

Then there's the matter of worldly possessions. Things are just things. But they carry meaning and memory. A parent with a dire prognosis might want to decide who gets what. That way, no arguments.

Liahona's mother is still alive but isn't sure how many years she will have. She wants to make sure that no one fights over her possessions if and when the time comes. Liahona, who's fourteen, describes her mom's solution: she made a list of all her jewelry and sent an email to the family to say who would get what.

"I'm glad she did it," Liahona says. "There are some things that I know are gonna be mine. I'm really happy I'll have them and I'll take good care of them." One thing she'll cherish is a necklace that spells out "I" and "L" and "Y" in sign language, for "I Love You." Wearing the necklace, Liahona believes, will keep her mother close to her in spirit.

HOT DOGS = BETTER THAN DISNEY WORLD?

You don't want to raise false hope, but "hope is an important thing to have," says social worker Bunty Anderson. You can hope for bright moments even at a time of uncertainty. And you may discover that the best laid plans don't always work out...but a magic moment can come when you least expect it.

• •

Erin's Story: The Best Chili Dog

Erin Leigh's dad had lung cancer and did not have such a great prognosis. Even though he and her mom were divorced and living in separate states, the family planned a trip to theme parks in Orlando. That turned out to be not such an uplifting occasion. "All of us were just tense," Erin remembers. "We knew the purpose of the trip but nobody really talked about it."

What does stand out is a visit to her dad's home in

Ohio. He loved to cook and bake, she says, "and he was great at it." She had always loved visiting him in the past because he'd prepare such delicious food. On this last visit to Ohio, she asked him to make a Coney Island—another name for a chili dog. Even though his own taste buds were not in great shape because of his chemo, he made Erin a Coney Island. "I know he wanted to make it out of love," she says. And that chili dog was delicious.

Guardianship: A Single Parent's Dilemma

When parents are divorced, and the parent with custody of the kids is dying of cancer, the children want to know: who will take care of us?

"I think people are often confused about the rules of guardianship," says psychiatrist Paula Rauch. "A lot of single parents think they can leave their kid to someone. You can't. Guardianship goes to the surviving parent."

If, say, Mom has custody and has been giving Dad a bad rap, now that Mom has cancer, the prospect of Dad's guardianship could raise concerns. "There's so much need for repair," says social worker Bunty Anderson. "That needs some professional guidance. [The situation is] too loaded and layered with too much emotion."

In some families, however, the noncustodial parent would not become the guardian. That parent might simply not be in the picture or might have a legal history that caused the loss of parental rights. Or the custodial parent may want to fight it out in court and name another guardian.

The question of guardianship will also arise if the other parent is deceased.

The teen shouldn't have to ask about future living arrangements. Mom or Dad, bring it up.

First, you need a plan. And making a plan might require more than a few conversations with other family members. Depending on the circumstances, an aunt or uncle or grandparent may not be capable of taking in your child.

You might decide to ask your kids for their input. Mom might say, "I'm really sick right now. I'm hoping to be okay but we need to make these plans about what to do if I die. We need to talk about who's going to take care of you," says social work professor Victoria Rizzo.

You don't want to ask their opinion if there really aren't different options. Paula Rauch cautions: "The worst case scenario is giving kids a fake choice."

Let's say you now have a plan. How do you share it with your child? If this task were to fall to her, Bunty Anderson says, she'd probably say to the kids: "You might worry about what will happen. I just want you to know that we've made a plan."

She'd name the guardian but wouldn't pile on the details—which bedroom would you get in Uncle Brian's house if he's the guardian? Then it's up to the teen to ask—or not ask. "It's kind of in their ballpark," she says. Tell them, "When you feel like talking, we'll talk more."

And she'd come back to the subject in a month or two, asking: "Have you given any thought to it?" But she wouldn't push: "If the kids say, 'No,' leave it be."

The Art of the Promise

You might be tempted to start making promises to your children: don't worry, no matter what the doctors say, I'll beat this cancer. I'll be there for you when you need me.

If the prognosis is not good, that promise may be impossible to keep. So what do you say as a parent?

"What on God's earth would any of us do in that situation?" asks Bunty Anderson. "It's heart-wrenching. You never, ever want to be in a situation where you have to make that promise to your child if you know you probably can't keep it."

You might tell your kids you're going to do everything in your power to stay well and be present at future milestones. But you also need to acknowledge that that might not happen. And then you might talk about being with the child in other ways: "I'll always be in your heart."

What if you rashly make promises out of the best of intent, promises that cannot be kept? Bianca, seventeen, remembers the promises her dad made as he was being treated for cancer. "He promised he'd be there for graduation, that he'd be there for my wedding day."

Then he passed away two weeks before Christmas. So not only would he not be there for Bianca's future milestones, but he ruined her favorite holiday.

But she's not angry that he made promises he couldn't keep. "I'm glad he made those promises," she says with the perspective of five years of hindsight. "If he hadn't, I would feel like he didn't love me."

(Chapter 13 offers suggestions to teens for dealing with the loss of a parent.)

The World after Cancer

You may not feel the same as you did Before Cancer. That could be true for your teens as well. They're older, they've possibly taken on new chores at home and become more independent. "They want to continue that freedom and independence. Teens who have been helpful during their parent's cancer have taken on new responsibilities and kind of stretched to be more independent," says Kathleen McCue. But you might want to reclaim the parenting role.

Tell your kids: "Let's negotiate what's reasonable and right and fair at this point in our lives as a family." Sit down and work it out.

Both of you may have to bend a little. Parents, maybe you can trust your teen a little more.

And you're likely to be different, too. Maybe you don't have as much energy. Maybe you need more emotional support.

Having another cancer-themed family meeting might be in order to talk about such issues. Elissa Bantug, whose mom was treated for cancer when Elissa was twelve, recalls a lack of "clear expectations of what was going to happen long term" after her mother finished treatment. She says there was "no conversation about survivorship and what that meant." All she knew was that "Mom wasn't going to jump back up and run around with us after treatment. She wasn't feeling well for a long time."

The other part of the "new normal" is keeping the experience as a part of your family. Talk to your kids. Listen to them. Eat dinner with them. Demand that they watch a movie with you every eleven months or so. And if parent and teen are having a tough time talking, go for a car ride and see if that helps bridge the communication gap.

THE FEAR IT MIGHT HAPPEN AGAIN

It's common for teens to be reluctant to visit the doctor themselves after a parent has had cancer. They may be afraid of getting bad news themselves.

Of her three now-grown children, cancer survivor and

physician Wendy Harpham says: "The oldest and youngest have more anxiety about physical issues than they would have otherwise, and it's more of a struggle for them to go to a doctor than if I'd never been sick."

We asked Harpham: "Do you nudge your kids gently about seeing a doctor?

"I nudge them directly," she answered.

She added, "I do not use guilt or manipulation. That really turns me off. The best thing we can do for our children [when they become adults] is to respect their autonomy."

There's also a worry that if you're in remission, the cancer could return.

If your teen asks, "Are you 100 percent sure it won't come back," what can you say?

Harpham's response: "The answer is, 'No. I wish I could be 100 percent sure. Part of me would like to say that. But what I can say is the doctors are confident that this treatment gives really good odds for a long life. And if things change, I'll tell you.'"

If your parent is dealing with metastatic disease that is being "managed"—with the hope of years ahead—the challenge is to keep communicating over the months (and we hope years) ahead.

Make a contract with your teen about the flow of information, suggests social worker Sara Goldberger. The key question: "How much do you want to know and when do you want to know it?" Does your teen want an update after every medical visit, or just bulletins when and if things change?

And if your teen asks you the awful question, *Will you die from this?*" oncologist Lidia Schapira suggests this kind of response: "Yes it's likely I will die of this, but I'm going to keep pushing that date back. I expect I'll be around for many years."

(What does the "new normal" mean for teens, and how can they make it work for them? Check out Chapter 14.)

RESOURCES

GROUPS AND ORGANIZATIONS

American Association of Caregiving Youth
aacy.org; 800-725-2512
AACY offers support for young people caring for a family member. The Florida headquarters and its affiliates run workshops that can help kids cope with household responsibilities. The website also has information and a resource list. In addition, AACY encourages young caregivers to call and share comments.

American Cancer Society
cancer.org; 800-227-2345
If you've got a question about cancer, this organization's thorough and up-to-date website will probably have the answer. The American Cancer Society also takes phone calls 24 hours a day on its toll-free number and can connect callers with local resources. All conversations are free and confidential.

Camp Kesem
campkesem.org
The camp, which takes its name from the Hebrew word for magic, welcomes kids ages six to sixteen who've faced a parent's cancer. The first Camp Kesem was held in 2000 and was sponsored by students at Stanford University. Today there are 40-plus Camp Kesems, with

more in the works. Each site is run by students at a local university and provides a free one-week camp stay for eligible youngsters. Last year, the camp hosted more than 2,100 campers; 400 of them were teens. *(See Appendix A, page 209, to read more about Camp Kesem.)*

Cancer Care, Inc.
cancercare.org; 800-813-4673
Cancer Care offers free counseling in Connecticut, New Jersey, and New York by oncology social workers, and can provide information about in-person, phone, or online support groups for teens.

Cancer Support Community
cancersupprtcommunity.org
This nonprofit group has fifty affiliates in addition to satellite offices and online support. Check the website to see if there's a chapter in your area, then touch base to inquire about support programs and services for teens. Cancer Support Community also administers a website for teens with cancer in the family and teens with cancer: *grouploop.org.*

Children's Bereavement Center, Miami
childbereavement.org
Children's Bereavement Center of South Texas
cbcst.org
Each of the nonprofit centers provides free peer support groups for teens who've lost a parent.

Claudia Mayer Cancer Resource Center
hcgh.org/cmcrc
Based in Columbia, Maryland, the center sponsors a support group for teens dealing with a parent's cancer.

The Gathering Place

touchedbycancer.org; 216-595-9546

With two locations in Cleveland, this nonprofit offers support groups for teenagers as well as individual counseling.

Gilda's Club

gildasclubnyc.org, gildasclubchicago.org, gildasclubseattle.org, gildasclubdetroit.org, and more

This cancer support group is named for the *Saturday Night Live* comic, Gilda Radner, who died of ovarian cancer. Clubs in cities across the United States offer programs for teens. The Seattle Gilda's Club and other chapters run an annual essay contest, called "It's Always Something," for teens affected by cancer in the family as well as teens who have been diagnosed with cancer. (See excerpts in Appendix B.)

H.O.P.E.

hopeforcancerfamilies.org; 717-227-2824

This Pennsylvania nonprofit's services include Kids Under Construction, which offers activities (and a chance to talk) for young people fighting cancer as well as youngsters dealing with a family member's cancer. The group also offers help with shopping, transportation, and other day-to-day needs.

HopeWell

hopewellcancersupport.org; 410-832-2719

The cancer center regularly runs six-week support groups for teens facing a parent's cancer. Teen Circle is for teens whose parent is going through treatment or dealing with its aftermath. Teen Grief Group addresses the loss of a parent to cancer. The groups meet in the group's Lutherville, Maryland, location, just outside Baltimore.

Kids Konnected

kidskonnected.org; 800-899-2866

The Orange County–based support group was founded in 1993 by thirteen-year-old Jon Wagner-Holtz, who wished for support when his own mom was dealing with breast cancer. With a grant from the Susan G. Komen foundation, he set up an 800 number that he answered from his bedroom. Today, Kids Konnected has a professional staff, four chapters in southern California, and branches in several states. Its teen programs, all in California, include year-round support groups, a Youth Leadership mentor program, and a weeklong summer camp with daytime activities like river rafting and archery and nightly support sessions.

Life with Cancer

lifewithcancer.org; 703-698-2526

Based in Fairfax, Virginia, this group offers support groups for teens coping with a parent's cancer as well as for teens who've lost a family member to the disease.

Livestrong

livestrong.org; 855-220-7777

This organization, founded by cancer survivor Lance Armstrong, offers one-on-one support for cancer survivors and their caregivers, family members, and friends. Call Livestrong or submit a request online at livestrong.org/gethelp. In addition, Livestrong offers opportunities to join in athletic events that raise funds to help fight cancer.

Marjorie E. Korff PACT Program
(Parenting At a Challenging Time)

mghpact.org; 617-724-7272

The program, based at the Massachusetts General Hospital Cancer Center, provides guidance for parents with cancer and their spouses or co-parents. Teens will likely find PACT a helpful resource as well.

MD Anderson Cancer Center

mdanderson.org; 713-792-6195

This world-renowned center, located in Houston, offers Teen Climb, a six-week program for teens who have a parent in treatment at MD Anderson. A parent program is offered during the same cycle. Call for information.

National Cancer Institute

cancer.gov; PDQ: cancer.gov/cancertopics/pdq

Part of the U.S. National Institutes of Health, NCI offers one of the most thorough and up-to-date websites on cancer. The site for PDQ, Physician Data Query, is a comprehensive database with information presented for both patients and physicians.

Sloan Kettering Cancer Center—Kids Express Program

mskcc.org; 212-639-7029

Kids Express helps kids during a parent's cancer treatment, providing brochures and referrals to therapists. Kids who have a parent in treatment at Sloan Kettering can call to speak to a social worker. Staff social workers also offer guidance to adult cancer patients about discussing the disease with their children.

Students of Survivors

studentsofsurvivors.org

This Alabama-based organization provides an annual scholarship to a teen who's had a parent diagnosed with cancer during the high school years.

SuperSibs

supersibs.org; in Illinois 847-462-4742, toll-free 888-417-4704

The group helps kids who have a sibling with cancer, but many of the teen issues discussed on its website are relevant to kids coping with a parent's cancer as well.

Susan G. Komen for the Cure
komen.org; 877-465-6636
Teens for the Cure—a program for teens who'd like to get involved in breast cancer awareness and fund-raising—is offered by chapters in Philadelphia, New York City, and El Paso, Texas. In Philly, the teens put on a fundraising fashion show called "Tickled Pink." Other chapters emphasize participation in the local Komen 5K race and bringing information about the disease to schools.

The Komen Scholarship Program offers college scholarships to teens who've lost a parent to breast cancer. Send an email to contactus@applyists.com for information.

Tu Nidito Children and Family Services
tunudito.org; 520-322-9155
Tu Nidito, Spanish for "your little nest," is a Tucson, Arizona, group that offers regular support group session for teens coping with a parent's cancer as well as groups for parents who've been diagnosed with the disease and caregiver parents.

BOOKS FOR PARENTS

These books offer superb guidance for parents.

How to Help Children Through a Parent's Serious Illness
    by Kathleen McCue and Ron Bonn (St. Martin's Griffin)

Raising an Emotionally Healthy Child When a Parent Is Sick: A Harvard Medical School Book
    by Paula Rauch and Anna Muriel (McGraw-Hill)

When a Parent Has Cancer: A Guide to Caring for Your Children
    by Wendy Schlessel Harpham (William Morrow)

ACKNOWLEDGMENTS

We are deeply grateful to the people who made this book possible. We spoke with dozens of extraordinary teenagers, who shared their time and insights. You are the heart and soul of this book. You keep it grounded in reality and added welcome (and sometimes dark) humor.

For bringing many great teens to meet us, we must thank Abby O'Leary, national program director for Camp Kesem. "Avocado," you are an organizational genius and you were exquisitely sensitive to all the issues in researching a book like this. We can't thank you enough! We are also deeply indebted to Kathleen McCue, who let us speak to two of the teen support groups she runs at the Gathering Place in Cleveland.

We also are in the debt of the doctors, therapists, social workers, and other professionals who took time from their busy lives to answer our questions. We wanted to offer special thanks to our go-to people, who fielded questions over the many months we spent on the book and always had wise answers: Seth Berkowitz, Anne Coscarelli, Barbara Golby, Sara Goldberger, Barry J. Jacobs, Kathleen McCue, Paula Rauch, and Jill Taylor-Brown.

A number of people read the manuscript and offered important suggestions: thank you one and all. We have to give a special shout out to Elissa Bantug for her helpful perspectives as both a teen whose mom had cancer and now as a cancer educator. Rick Ogden, your comments from both a professional and personal perspective, were spot-on. Kathleen McCue and Seth Berkowitz, your edits were invaluable.

To our teen reader, Jackie Shmock—many thanks for your kind words!

There would have been no book without the vision of Anna Gottlieb, a wonderful friend and the director of Gilda's Club Seattle, who sent us essays written by teens about a parent's cancer, from her group's annual essay contest, and said, "There has to be a book you can do."

This book would never have been published without the extraordinary efforts of our agent, Lindsay Edgecombe, who truly believed in the project. Thank you, Lindsay! And we are deeply grateful for the support and guidance from our excellent editor Leah Hultenschmidt and the entire team at Sourcebooks.

Special thanks from Marc to Marsha, for putting up with my absentee husbandism while I was reporting and writing, to my mother for inspiring me with her courage and good humor, to my supportive and wonderful colleagues at National Geographic, especially Victoria Pope, Maggie Zackowitz (for leading me to Camp Kesem), and gifted copy editor Cindy Leitner. And to dear daughter Daniela, who gave me words of support and private yoga classes when I needed a moment of zen, and to the best coauthor I could imagine: Maya!

Special thanks from Maya to Daniela, who provided camaraderie during this experience, provided insights and ideas for this guide, tolerated my grumpiness during the writing, and is the best sister in the west. Thanks to Casey for printing out the entire manuscript and reading it thoroughly with a red pen and making sure we warned teens that if they punch walls (which we definitely do not recommend doing), they should watch out for studs so they don't break their hands.

Thank you to the following people who provided their expertise and guidance:

Bunty Anderson, BSW, family counselor, CancerCare Manitoba, Winnipeg

Elissa Bantug, MHS, program coordinator, Breast Cancer Survivorship Program, the Johns Hopkins Sidney Kimmel Comprehensive Cancer Center, Baltimore

Seth Berkowitz, LCSW, CCLS, patient services manager, Southern Florida Chapter, the Leukemia & Lymphoma Society, Hollywood, Florida

Suzanne Brace, executive director, HopeWell Cancer Support, Baltimore

Monica Coreman, MA, PCC, grief counselor, Hospice of the Western Reserve, Cleveland

Anne Coscarelli, Ph.D., psychologist and founding director of the Simms/Mann – UCLA Center for Integrative Oncology at UCLA's Jonsson Comprehensive Cancer Center, David Geffen School of Medicine, Los Angeles

Maureen Davey, Ph.D., LMFT, Assistant Professor, Drexel University, College of Nursing and Health Professions, Department of Couple and Family Therapy, Philadelphia

Jenny Eckert, LCSW, OSW-C, RPT, Program Manager, Life with Cancer, Fairfax, Virginia

Michael Eselun, Chaplain, Simms/Mann – UCLA Center for Integrative Oncology, Los Angeles

Melissa A. Ford, LMSW, school social worker, Area Education Agency 267, Grinnell, Iowa

Anna Franklin, MD, assistant professor in the Department of Pediatrics at the Children's Cancer Hospital, University of Texas MD Anderson Cancer Center, Houston

Barbara Golby, LCSW, clinical social worker, Memorial Sloan-Kettering Cancer Center, New York

Sara Goldberger, LCSW-R, senior director, program, Cancer Support Community, New York

James Gordon, MD, psychiatrist, founder, and director of the Center for Mind-Body Medicine, Washington, D.C., author of *Your Guide to the Seven-Stage Journey Out of Depression*

Mae Greenberg, LMHC, mental health counselor, Cancer Support Community, Miami

April Greene, MSSW, LCSW, social work counselor, University of Texas MD Anderson Cancer Center, Houston

Wendy Griffith, MCCW, LCSW, social work counselor, University of Texas MD Anderson Cancer Center, Houston

The Reverend George Handzo, M.Div., senior consultant for chaplaincy care and practice at HealthCare Chaplaincy in New York and past director, chaplaincy services, Memorial Sloan-Kettering Cancer Center

Mary Hardy, MD, medical director of the Simms/Mann-UCLA Center for Integrative Medicine, Los Angeles

Wendy Harpham, MD, physician/survivor, Dallas, who has written and lectured extensively on getting good care and living as fully as possible after cancer

Yusuf Hasan, pediatric chaplain, Memorial Sloan-Kettering Cancer Center, New York

Barry J. Jacobs, Psy.D., clinical psychologist, Springfield, Pennsylvania, and author of *The Emotional Survival Guide for Caregivers: Looking After Yourself and Your Family While Helping an Aging Parent*

Shavaun Jones, M.Ed., P.C., children's bereavement counselor, Hospice of the Western Reserve, Cleveland

Cynthia Lofaso, Ph.D., professor of psychology at Central Virginia Community College and therapist for Camp Kesem's Virginia site

Kathleen McCue, LSW, CCLS, child life specialist and director, Children's Program, at the Gathering Place in Cleveland, Ohio

Marisa Minor, LCSW, social worker, University of Texas MD Anderson Cancer Center, Houston

Richard Ogden, Ph.D., psychologist, Bethesda, Maryland

Cheryl Olson, Sc.D., public health researcher, Reston, Virginia; and cofounder of the Center for Mental Health and Media at Harvard Medical School

Paula Rauch, MD, child psychiatrist and director of the Marjorie E. Korff PACT Program (Parenting At a Challenging Time), Massachusetts General Hospital, Boston

Sandra K. Ring, MS, CCLS, national director of outreach and education, SuperSibs!, headquartered outside of Chicago

Victoria M. Rizzo, MSW, LCSW-R, Ph.D., assistant professor and Hartford Geriatric Social Work Faculty Scholar, Columbia University School of Social Work, New York

Lidia Schapira, MD, assistant professor of medicine, Harvard Medical School, Boston

Richard Sloan, Ph.D., professor of behavioral medicine, Columbia University Medical Center, New York

Shara Sosa, MSW, LCSW, oncology counselor, Life with Cancer, Fairfax, Virginia

Jill Taylor-Brown, MSW, RSW, social worker and director, patient and family support services, CancerCare Manitoba, Winnipeg

Eliezer M. Van Allen, MD, Fellow in Medical Oncology at Dana-Farber/Partners Cancer Care, Boston; cofounder of Camp Kesem-UCLA and advisory board member for Camp Kesem-MIT

Karen Weihs, MD, psychiatrist and Medical Director for Supportive Care, University of Arizona Cancer Center, Tucson

Marisa Weiss, MD, breast cancer oncologist, Philadelphia area; founder of breastcancer.org, coauthor with her daughter Isabel Friedman of *Taking Care of Your "Girls": A Breast Health Guide for Girls, Teens, and In-Betweens*

Ricia Wiener, Ph.D., school psychologist, Washington-Lee High School, Arlington, Virginia

Lynnette Wilhardt, LCSW, director of clinical services, Kids Konnected, San Diego

About the Authors

Marc Silver is an editor at *National Geographic* magazine and the author of *Breast Cancer Husband: How to Help Your Wife (and Yourself) Through Diagnosis, Treatment, and Beyond*, written after his wife, Marsha, was diagnosed with breast cancer. Today, Marsha is in good health. She and Marc live in Chevy Chase, Maryland, and are the proud parents of Maya and Daniela. Writing this book helped Marc reconnect with his "inner teen."

Maya Silver lives in Crested Butte, Colorado, where she works as the Executive Director of the Office for Resource Efficiency and plays in the mountains. She won the Diane Vreuls Fiction Prize at Oberlin College in 2008 and has contributed to *U.S. News & World Report* and *Washington Post Express*. She was fifteen when her mom was diagnosed with cancer.